The Rain Whisperer

Essays on finding joy in every storm

THE RAIN WHISPERER

WHISPERER

ESSAYS ON FINDING JOY IN EVERY STORM

Christina Madonia-Knisley

ISBN: 979-8-9992274-1-6

To my family and friends.

For your love, laughter and unwavering support that have shaped these pages and carried me through every storm. Your kindness, humor and steady presence mean more than words can express.

I am forever grateful.

Table of Contents

'Look at the rain long enough, with no thoughts in your head, and you gradually feel your body falling loose, shaking free of the world of reality.'

— Haruki Murakami,
South of the Border, West of the Sun

'...I don't just wish you rain, Beloved - I wish you the beauty of storms...'

— John Geddes,
A Familiar Rain

Preface

This book started with a storm. Not the poetic kind or a symbolic crisis—but a real, blindsiding, life-upending, out-of-the-deepest-blue kind of storm. A lung cancer diagnosis. ALK-positive, to be exact. One day I was just living my life, and the next, I was thrown into a world of scans, meds, appointments, and the constant hum of 'What now?'

At first, I wrote to just to stay sane. I needed a place to put everything—my fears, my frustration, and the surprisingly funny moments that still managed to sneak in. Writing became a kind of lifeline, a way to make sense of the chaos. But over time, it turned into something else. Something healing. Something beautiful.

What you'll find in these pages isn't just about cancer. It's about life—small-town life, real life, messy life. It's about the ridiculous things people say, the quiet grace that shows up when you least expect it, and the odd magic of laughing through tears. It's not always neat, but it's honest.

The Rain Whisperer is a celebration of the human spirit's remarkable ability to find joy and hope in the midst of adversity. I invite you to walk with me through these pages, to find solace in shared experience, and to listen to the subtle whispers of wisdom carried in every drop of rain. Let's find the laughter that makes the storm worth weathering.

As Vivian Greene said, 'Life isn't about waiting for the storm to pass. It's about learning how to dance in the rain.'

PART ONE:

THE MOMENT THE MAP CAUGHT FIRE

I was minding my own business.

Which, for me, meant wrangling words at Blair—a retail catalog that's survived since 1910 by selling elastic waistbands, velour leisure suits and enough sensible shoes to outfit a small army. It meant loving my loud, unpredictable life, reinventing myself for the twentieth (okay, maybe thirtieth) time, and waking up most mornings with either a half-baked dream, a fresh existential crisis, or an uninvited farm animal staring at me from the porch.

I was fifty-six, married to a man I adore—a creature of pure goodness who has the heart of a golden retriever, the bravery of a mastiff, and the loyalty of Velcro. His name is Wes, but around here we call him 'the man who says yes to everything except corn.' I have raised three humans to adulthood, none of whom were arrested in the process, which I consider a personal win. And somewhere along the way, I accidentally became the kind of person who finds humor in almost anything—except ants. I draw the line at ants. Tiny foot soldiers of terror. I will burn a house down before I let them win.

So yes, life was rolling along. Not perfectly. Not according to any five-year plan. But beautifully. In that messy, ordinary, completely extraordinary way.

One day, I woke up and decided to raise alpacas (as one sometimes does), and by sundown we had bought a 20-acre farm and were knee-deep in hay and hopes. We called it *Bella Luna Alpaca Farm*. There lived fainting goats, emus, chickens, turkeys—basically the cast of a rural fever dream. We turned a toolshed into an Airbnb and welcomed guests from all over the world. City people who had

FORECAST: UNHINGED

My mood swings with the weather.
If it's sunny, I cry in the laundry room.
If it's raining, I bake cookies.
If it's partly cloudy?
I buy alpacas.

never touched a fluffy animal would leave misty-eyed, vowing to start farms of their own. It was magical. We eventually sold the farm, but kept a sweet little four-acre plot where our Amish friends helped us build a cabin that overlooks a one-horse town with no stoplights and one highly suspect Dollar General. It was our retirement dream. And I thought, genuinely, 'Life is good.'

Sure, I had a nagging cough. But who doesn't? I chalked it up to post-nasal drip, allergies, possibly karma for mocking those who take elderberry supplements. Nothing serious. Until Labor Day weekend. That's when the cough ramped up and my chest began to ache—like I'd bench-pressed a toddler-sized alpaca and forgotten about it.

Reluctantly (and only because Wes gave me *that* look), I went to the ER. I figured they'd give me antibiotics and a gentle reminder to drink water and stop Googling. But instead, after hours of tests and scans and hushed hallway conferences, a very kind doctor walked into my room and said the sentence that would quietly detonate my entire existence:

'Your heart checked out okay... but there's a sizable nodule in your right lung.' *And that was it.*

The words hung in the air like a cloud of smoke. Everything before that moment went quiet—my thoughts, my plans, my sense of who I was. It all paused, like someone had hit the mute button on my life. One week later, I was lying in a surgical suite at the Cleveland Clinic having a bronchoscopy, and later that day, I had a name for the thing that had sneaked in without permission: Stage 3a ALK+ lung cancer.

And just like that, the map, the one I had spent a lifetime sketching in journals and dreams and endless lists, caught fire.

Nothing made sense anymore. Not the diagnosis. Not the timeline. Not the fact that I had *just* bought organic chicken broth in bulk. Not the years I spent reinventing myself with positive mantras and self-help books. Not plans for the cabin, or the books I wanted to write, or the big birthdays I hadn't yet celebrated.

It was the most bizarre kind of theft—not just of breath, but of direction. Of momentum. Of certainty.

One moment I was Christina, lover of rain and ringleader of mildly chaotic joy, and the next, I was a patient. A statistic. A number on a chart.

And this was the moment the storm rolled in. The thunder before the chapters to come. The unraveling that would strip me to the core.

In the face of the trauma, I wasn't brave or resilient or anything you'd find on an inspirational coffee mug. I could barely breathe—literally and emotionally. I was stunned, hollowed out, like someone had pressed pause on my whole life and forgotten to hit play again.

But first, I had to sit in the silence... and learn how to be lost.

CHAPTER 1: GRIEVING THE PERSON I USED TO BE

I used to think grief was something reserved for funerals and casseroles. For widows and orphans. For the empty chair at Thanksgiving or the unanswered phone call that will never be returned. Grief was for the visible losses—the kind people nod solemnly at and send flowers for.

But it turns out, you can grieve a version of yourself, too.

It hit me like a rogue wave. One minute I was scrolling through my ALK+ support group, and the next, I was breathless, wrecked by one sentence someone casually typed into the thread:

'We are mourning who we used to be—people without cancer.'

And just like that, the wild mood swings, the unprovoked tears, the simmering rage at commercial jingles and cheerful weather reports— they all made sense.

I wasn't just sick. I was in mourning.

Not for someone else.

For *me*.

DENIAL AND SHOCK: THIS ISN'T HAPPENING

When the doctor said, *'There's a sizable nodule in your right lung,'* I actually looked around the room like maybe he was reading someone else's chart and had wandered into the wrong dimension. Lung cancer? No. Not possible. That happens to people on billboards. People who have a pack-a-day habit and a tragic backstory. Not to me—a middle-aged alpaca enthusiast with a fondness for coffee creamer and zero lung symptoms, besides a nagging cough I'd been brushing off for months.

In the days that followed, I clung to magical thinking like it was a security blanket. The doctors would fix it. I'd go back to normal. I'd have a quirky little scar, maybe write a few funny essays, and move on. Cancer wouldn't dare mess with someone as busy as me.

Spoiler alert: It dared.

ANGER: HOW DARE THIS HAPPEN TO ME?

Once the denial started to fade, the rage rolled in. Not the Hollywood kind, where you smash plates and scream into the abyss. Mine was more... simmering. Sharp. Sarcastic. It showed up in muttered curses and irrational hatred toward overly cheerful strangers. It showed up in how I snapped at people who told me to 'stay positive' as if positivity were some kind of cancer bleach that I could just buy.

I raged at the randomness of it all.

At the couples holding hands in grocery-store aisles.

At people who booked vacations without checking their scan schedule first.

At anyone who dared to breathe effortlessly.

It felt as if life had personally betrayed me—and then had the audacity to keep spinning like nothing happened.

THE
GRIEF
GUEST

Grief came in uninvited.
Didn't knock.
Tracked in mud.
Rearranged my furniture.
And worst of all—
made itself comfortable
with my company.

BARGAINING: IF I DO EVERYTHING RIGHT...

This is the phase where I became a PhD-level Googler. I was suddenly fluent in terms like 'alk-inhibitor' and 'anti-inflammatory protocol' and had opinions on sea moss. I loaded my cart with turmeric, elderberry, beet juice, and things I couldn't pronounce but which *definitely* sounded curative.

I tried to outsmart fate.

If I only ate clean.

If I only stayed calm.

If I only meditated with the devotion of a monk while drinking spinach sludge through a bamboo straw...

Maybe I could trade my way out of this.

I whispered silent deals to the universe. I offered up my fear in exchange for remission. I begged without realizing I was bargaining, just hoping the old me might come back if I played by new rules. I was desperate to find my way back to life as I knew it. Somehow. Anyhow.

DEPRESSION: THE WEIGHT OF REALITY

Eventually, I sank.

I didn't recognize myself anymore—not in the mirror, not in my thoughts. I was tired in a way that didn't lift with naps or nice weather. There were days I didn't want to talk. Days I didn't want to hope.

Cancer didn't just show up in my lungs. It unpacked its emotional baggage all over my life. It took up space in my calendar, my dreams, my language. I couldn't even make plans without attaching a footnote:

if I'm feeling up to it.

if my scan is clean.

if I'm still here.

The heaviness wasn't always loud. Sometimes it was just this quiet ache that I carried everywhere...missing the person I used to be. The one who didn't flinch when her phone rang with an unknown number. The one who didn't know words like 'progression' or 'biomarker.' The one who didn't wake up every day wondering how many days I had in the bank.

ACCEPTANCE: SOMEONE NEW IS EMERGING

Here's the hardest truth: She's gone.

That version of me—the carefree, unscarred one—doesn't exist anymore.

But here's the softer truth: I'm still here.

Acceptance doesn't arrive with a triumphant theme song. It sneaks in quietly, like a neighbor with soup. It's noticing the small moments that don't feel heavy. It's a belly laugh that doesn't feel borrowed. A walk that doesn't end in exhaustion. A moment of peace where fear didn't interrupt.

I still grieve the old me.

But I'm learning to care for this new version: this woman who is raw and real and entirely reassembled.

She's still silly. She almost always laughs at inappropriate moments. She still hates ants and adores alpacas and loves a good metaphor.

No, I haven't made full peace with it. Some days I cycle through all five stages before lunch. But I'm learning to live in the space between loss and becoming. To be present. To breathe again. To find joy, not in who I was, but in who I *still* am.

And maybe most of all, I've learned that buried under the panic and disbelief, a tiny flicker of my old self managed to whisper:

Well, this is inconvenient. I just started using retinol.

CHAPTER 2: THE BIG, BAD BIKER GANG IN MY BODY

Yesterday, I got the golden acronym: NED.

No Evidence of Disease.

I let that sink in. I felt a wave of relief. I thanked God, my doctors, the universe, my family, all dogs, the academy and anyone else taking requests. Because if you're living with ALK-positive lung cancer, getting NED isn't just good news—it's the holy grail of oncology appointments.

Hearing those words should feel like crossing a finish line, right? Balloons, confetti, a heartfelt montage with uplifting music. But with ALK-positive lung cancer, NED isn't a victory parade—it's more like a temporary ceasefire. It doesn't mean the enemy is gone. It just means they've gone *undetectable*. For now.

Because ALK doesn't play by traditional rules. It's not the kind of cancer you treat once and forget. It's a sneaky, stubborn genetic mutation that can lie low, regroup, and then reappear like a spark in dry brush—unpredictable and fast. That's why I still have to show up for regular scans as though I'm checking in with airport security for a flight that might not even take off. I'm living in the uneasy pause between alarms, trying to act normal while knowing that a microscopic riot could break out at any moment.

So yes, I'm NED. But this story isn't over.

The gang is still out there, somewhere.

And I say this *not* to sound ungrateful, or to be a downer, but to be real about what this journey actually looks like. ALK+ lung cancer isn't your regular, run-of-the-mill tumor situation. It doesn't just *come back*. It comes back like a big, bad, leather-clad, weapon-wielding motorcycle gang, and when it does, it means business.

THE ALK+ OUTLAWS: A BIKER GANG THAT WON'T QUIT

ALK+ cancer cells aren't content with just hanging out quietly in some forgotten corner of my body. No, these jerks are the kind that love to stir up trouble. Most of the time, they roam around individually, laying low, maybe revving their engines just to remind me they exist. But then, one day, they decide it's time for a rally.

And not just any rally—a full-blown, lawless, Sturgis-sized, chaos-inducing cancer riot.

Suddenly, the individual gang members start rolling into town, merging together in one big, stupid, menacing mass. They slap on more leather, they upgrade their weapons, and they recruit even more unruly members to their cause. They set up shop in some unfortunate organ, light a few metaphorical fires, and start raising absolute hell.

That's when the TKIs—the targeted therapy drugs like Alectinib—get the call.

THE SPECIAL FORCES: TARGETED THERAPY HITS BACK

So, ALK+ cancer is the relentless biker gang, and TKIs are the elite Special Forces unit sent in to take them down. These meds don't just roll up with a couple of flashlights and a stern warning. No, they pick out the gang members one by one. They move with precision, tracking down these cancerous punks and neutralizing them.

And this *really* pisses the gang off. The remaining gang members hate being taken out. So, naturally, they call for backup. More members ride in, stronger and even more defiant than before. They learn the Special Forces' tactics, adapt and get harder to defeat. The TKIs switch up their strategy, new reinforcements arrive, and the cycle continues—this exhausting, high-stakes game of destruction and defense.

WHY NED ISN'T THE FINISHLINE

So, while I am grateful beyond words for my NED status today, I also know the truth: this is a battle that just doesn't end. This isn't a one-and-done victory. The gang is still out there. They're scattered, regrouping, waiting for the next opportunity.

And that's why I have to stay on my medication, side effects and all. That's why I have to keep showing up for scans, watching and waiting, living in the disquiet between the 3-month check ins. That's why I don't get to close this chapter, at least not yet.

But here's the thing.

I'm not an extra in this story; I'm the main character. And I've got my own arsenal: humor, grit, good doctors, a fierce support system, and an irrationally deep love of rainy days. So no, I won't live in fear of the next riot these cells might stage. I'll take this reprieve for what it is: a breath, a gift, a moment to celebrate the fact that I'm still here.

The biker gang may come back.

But so will my Special Forces.

And trust me, they'll be ready.

CHAPTER 3: FILLING THE SPACE BETWEEN THE 3'S

Three months. Ninety days. Twelve weeks. However I choose to count them, they all lead to the same place—the next scan.

ALK-positive lung cancer dictates living in three-month increments, measured by the space between scans. Every twelve weeks, my body undergoes a full evaluation, searching for signs of the cancer's return—its inevitable, eager attempt to reclaim its territory. My new medication, Alectinib, is designed to hold the line, to keep the battle in check, but it comes with its own trials—side effects that read like the fine print of a dystopian novel and a price tag that could purchase a small island. Over $20,000 a month to keep me here, walking, writing, living.

Today is the first of many '3's.' I return to Cleveland Clinic for scans following three months of chemotherapy. The words I long to hear are simple: No Evidence of Disease—NED, the golden acronym of hope. But this is just one milestone in a long journey, a game of endurance where the finish line constantly shifts. Today marks the start of the next cycle, the next stretch of time where the waiting begins again.

And therein lies the challenge.

HOW DO I FILL THE SPACE BETWEEN THE 3'S?

Often, I allow these waiting periods to be ruled by angst and apprehension. The in-between days become footnotes to the next scan, moments that pass without truly being lived. I want to learn how to embrace the days in between, to see them for what they are—not just a countdown, but time itself. I want to find a way to be present, to stop marking my life in increments of fear.

This is the work of the journey.

I don't have a road map for this yet. Maybe I'll find solace in writing, in laughter, in the way rain taps against the window on an otherwise ordinary afternoon. Maybe I'll steal moments of peace in doggie snuggles, in watching Wes do something funny, in the magic of a hot cup of tea. Maybe I'll simply learn to breathe, without waiting for the next breath to be stolen by worry.

The space between the 3's is mine to fill.

SOFT REBUILDING

I fell apart so gently
you'd never know I broke.
I smiled between the splinters,
cracked jokes beneath the smoke.
Now piece by patient piece,
I glue myself with grace—
A softer kind of strength
in every tender place.

CHAPTER 4: WHY MY TO-DO LIST IS MORE FICTION THAN REALITY

Ah, the to-do list. That sacred scroll of intentions, half-baked dreams, and delusions of productivity. Every Sunday evening, armed with a fresh pen and an unhealthy level of optimism, I sit down to craft my week's masterpiece: the ultimate to-do list. (Not really. But I *think* about it. And that counts for something.)

It's never just a list; it's a novel—a Choose Your Own Adventure for the delusional overachiever.

Take this week, for example. Here's a taste of my top-tier fantasy zone:

Bake a croquembouche for absolutely no reason. Because nothing screams 'I've got my life together' like building a towering pyramid of cream-filled pastry puffs and gluing them together with homemade, scalding-hot caramel. (Fun fact: you can make caramel by simmering an unopened can of sweetened condensed milk for three hours. Is this safe? Probably not. Is it on my list? Absolutely.)

Visit Churchill, Manitoba, to kiss a polar bear on the nose. It always seems like my Best Idea Ever at 1:30 a.m. when I'm wide awake, angst-ridden by the vast majority of my life's poor decisions. 'You know what I REALLY need? Polar bear noses. That'll fix everything.'

Train Tucker to bring me stuff (or to do anything). He's a goldendoodle. But I refuse to give up on the dream of a dog made-to-order-and-delivered sandwich. Current progress: he stares at me, and says, 'Why won't you let me out? Why won't you feed me? Why don't you love me? It's the only thing in my life that matters. Unlike whatever that is you're doing—seriously, it looks pointless.'

Write a heartfelt thank-you note to the beach. 'Dear beach, I love you. Thank you for transforming my negative, chaotic energy into unfiltered tranquility. I don't know how you do it, but one minute I'm a hot mess, and the next, I'm lying in your sand like a comatose starfish. You're not just a vacation destination; you're my official therapist. So, thanks for always being there, even if you occasionally sneak sand into places sand has no business being.' Sentiment = genuine. Execution = still pending, finding the beach's official address.

Invent a new dance called 'The Roundabout Shuffle'. Inspired by my town's new traffic circle, it involves a lot of spinning in place, flailing dramatically, and yielding to imaginary dancers on your left. Sweeping TikTok stardom is inevitable. Unfortunately, I can't dance.

Organize the spice rack alphabetically... in Latin. Why stop at 'cinnamon' when I can search endlessly for 'Cinnamomum verum'? Invent a buyer's remorse app. This app would prohibit me from ordering anything from Amazon unless, of course, it's stuff 'I need', which I would qualify as anything I order on Amazon, thus nullifying the app's usefulness.

Meditate for thirty minutes every day. This sounds wholesome in theory but just results in me trying to Zen my way out of meditating.

Finally read War and Peace. Or at least carry it around in public. Reality check: I've been stuck on the title page since 1985.

And so, as my weeks in recovery roll on, my imaginary to-do list morphs from a hopeful road map into a tragic comedy. In reality, I frantically scribble realistic goals like:

Drink water

Nap

Don't trip over the dogs

MiraLAX!

The list is covered in coffee rings, cookie crumbs, half-finished tasks and the faint outline of my forehead from where I've face-planted onto the counter.

There's a little magic in the fiction of it all. Sure, I'll probably never kiss a polar bear on the nose or train Tucker to do the dishes, but it's productive to think I might.

Besides, if I ever do invent 'The Roundabout Shuffle,' you'll be the first to know.

THE ASHES WHISPERED

I wasn't ruined.
I was reworked.
The fire didn't finish me—
it forged me.
And the ashes whispered,
'Start from here.'

CHAPTER 5: STACKED PLATES AND SUBTLE SHIFTS

Sometimes, losing who you are doesn't arrive with sirens or spotlights. It doesn't knock on the door carrying a flashing sign that says, 'WARNING: Identity shift in progress!' Sometimes, it sneaks in quietly. Like dishes.

Piled high.

Avoided longer than you'd care to admit.

Stacked like domestic Jenga, each layer a subtle reminder that something inside has gone a little off-track.

Before cancer, I was a doer. A make-it-happen-er. A woman who liked things mostly tidy, who found a weird sense of calm in a cleared countertop, even if the laundry had unionized in the corner. But somewhere between scans and side effects and emotional whiplash, I stopped noticing the little things. The things that once made me feel like myself became optional... and then impossible... and then, eventually, invisible.

That's the sneaky part of illness. It rarely bulldozes through your life in one grand, cinematic moment. It chips away slowly, rearranging your insides while the outside looks deceptively normal. The house still stands. But the person who is going through it? She starts to blur around the edges.

This isn't really about dishes. (Okay, maybe a little.) It's about how a sink full of crusty plates once felt like failure, until I realized it was also a breadcrumb trail. A quiet, sticky, slightly smelly map back to myself.

FROM MOLDY DISHES TO MODERN MIRACLES

Let's start with the greatest happy accident in medical history: the discovery of penicillin. As the story goes—à la my scientific recount—Alexander Fleming, a Scottish bloke clearly skilled at avoiding housecleaning and personal accountability, left his dirty petri dishes out while he went on vacation. Upon returning, he discovered a random blob of mold that had gone full Rambo on a colony of bacteria.

Now, here's where the story gets weird. Did Fleming think, 'Whit! This wee mold is gonnae change the world!' Of course not. His first thought was probably, 'What's that smell that's geein me the boak?' But then, because scientists are rather curious fellows, he poked around a bit and realized this mold had impressive bacteria-slaying powers. He named it penicillin, which is Latin for ' A magical moldy juice discovered by some Scottish bloke who didn't wash his dishes.'

So why am I talking about moldy dishes when my purpose is to talk about cancer medicine? Because, friends, I am convinced the same chaotic energy that led to penicillin is alive and well in modern oncology. Somewhere in a lab, a brilliant researcher knocked over their kombucha, stared at the mess for a wee bit too long, and proclaimed, 'What if...'

Enter Tyrosine Kinase Inhibitors (TKIs). These meds are like bouncers at Club Cancer, trained to block shady cellular substances that direct cancer cells to grow and divide faster than a middle-school rumor. They work by throwing a tantrum at ALL of your cells and then saying, 'Oh, but I didn't mean all of you, darlings!' It's a finely tuned dance between life and death, a masterpiece of repeatedly pushing you to the brink and snatching you back just in time to do it all again. Enter Cisplatin, Carboplatin, and Alectinib, my personal trio of frenemies.

Cisplatin is the diva of my personal treatment plan. It kills cancer, sure, but not without making a scene. Created in a lab somewhere in Europe by some guy called Dr Meltdown von Boom, who hypothesized, 'What if we weaponized platinum?,' Cisplatin works by damaging DNA so thoroughly that cancer cells (and innocent bystanders) give up and die. It's like the pink slip of the chemo world: blunt, effective, and leaves everyone feeling dramatically queasy.

Side effects? Oh, the standard nausea, fatigue, kidney failure, neuropathy, hair loss and an unshakable suspicion that it actually is licensed to kill.

Carboplatin is like Cisplatin's chill cousin. Where Cisplatin shows up in shiny sequins and squeals 'I'm the main character!', Carboplatin rolls in wearing sweatpants and says, 'Look, I'll do the same job, but without the dramatic zoom-in and reverberating background music.'

It's less toxic, which is nice, but don't be fooled—it's still platinum-based and wants to mess you up. It's like adopting a bear cub instead of a full-grown grizzly. Cute for a moment, but it will bite your face off eventually.

Now we get to Alectinib. Not your average TKI, this is more like an assassin than a grenade. Alectinib says, 'Why destroy the whole mob when I can take out the Boss?' It targets cancer cells with specific genetic mutations, making it the Elliott Ness of cancer meds: precise, brilliant, and occasionally insufferable.

The catch? It doesn't play fair. Side effects include weird muscle aches, headaches, difficulty moving, walking or breathing and the sense that it is quietly judging your Netflix choices. But hey, if it means fewer cells are collateral damage, I'll take it.

THE FUTURE OF CHEMO: ENTER PLUTONIUM PILLS?

If we've learned anything from the mad geniuses behind cancer medications, it's that nothing is off the table. Platinum-based drugs?

Sure, why not. Kombucha mutations? Absolutely. Which leads me to wonder: what's next?

Picture it—2030. Scientists, in glowing hazmat suits, unveil the next big thing: plutonium-based TKIs. Why stop at platinum when you can up the ante with a little radioactive flair? They'll call it *Plutolastin™: Powerful. Unforgiving. Glowing.*

Side effects? Oh, just a mild case of becoming your own nightlight and it might make your hair fall out again, but at least you'll save on electricity. But let's be real, if it promises to be even 10 percent better at killing cancer, I'll sign up and ask, 'Where do I recharge?'

Whatever it is, I'm game. I'll be here, clinging to the hope that science will keep saving the day with the just the right dose of chaos. After all, if penicillin can come from mold, who's saying the next miracle won't come from, oh, I don't know, a scientist sneezing on a microchip?

PART TWO:
NEEDLES, NAUSEA AND NON-SENSE

IN WHICH I ENTER THE MEDICAL SYSTEM AND PROMPTLY LOSE MY DIGNITY, MY APPETITE, AND ANY FAITH IN HOSPITAL GOWNS.

Illness, for the record, is not graceful.

It does not whisper politely or or wait its turn. It crashes in like a drunk party guest with bad timing and worse intentions. And once you're officially labeled a 'patient', you don't just lose your health. You lose logic, comfort, modesty, schedules, normalcy and sometimes... your actual pants.

Welcome to the middle of the story. The part where the body goes bonkers, the medical system collapses under its own clipboard and humor becomes a full-blown survival strategy.

This is the glorious, maddening, what-fresh-hell-is-this stage of chronic illness. The one where you spend your days navigating insurance phone trees, decoding side effects written by a gremlin and keeping your oncologist on their toes with questions like, 'What are your thoughts on Ivermectin?'

You'll find essays here that try to make sense of the senseless. It's chaotic. It's clinical. It's weirdly hilarious. And through it all, somehow, we keep our chin up and bash on regardless.

Because if I've learned anything from navigating this circus in a hospital gown that doesn't know how to tie properly, it's this:

Laughter is the one prescription nothing can't screw up.

CHAPTER 6: HOW TO MAKE YOUR ONCOLOGIST'S HEAD EXPLODE WITH ONE WORD

I consider myself a fairly reasonable person. I follow medical advice (mostly). I take my meds, show up for scans, and generally try not to drive my doctors insane. But I recently discovered that if you ever want to see a well-mannered, highly educated oncologist transform from a calm professional into a fire-breathing dragon in real time, just casually drop one word into the conversation: *Ivermectin*.

Nothing—*nothing*—will make a doctor's head explode faster. It's a secret code word that instantly triggers a reaction so intense, you'd think you just asked them if drinking bleach was a viable cancer treatment.

IVERMECTIN: PARASITE SLAYER, PROFESSIONAL RAGE INDUCER

Now, for those unfamiliar, ivermectin is an antiparasitic drug (I know, fancy words). It's been around for ages, curing all sorts of actual parasite infestations, including river blindness, elephantiasis, and scabies. And if that weren't impressive enough, some kombucha-drinking scientists suggest that ivermectin might have anticancer properties, potentially stopping tumor cells in their tracks.

Boom! Mind-blowing, right?

But do not—I repeat, do not—mention this to your oncologist unless you're prepared for a scene that will rival a live-action Looney Tunes episode.

THE GREAT IVERMECTIN DIVIDE: HOW TO IGNITE INSTANT CHAOS

Here's the backstory: Ivermectin used to be (and still is) a respectable, hard-working drug, minding its own business and curing worm-related misfortunes on happy farm animals everywhere. But then, COVID happened. Cue the controversy.

Some conservative media figures latched onto ivermectin as a cheap and effective COVID treatment, despite the FDA and the WHO basically screaming, 'For the love of all that is holy, please don't do this.' The official stance? Ivermectin is useless unless you're a horse and potentially dangerous in high doses. The counter-stance? Some doctors and public figures championed it as a miracle drug that was purposely being suppressed because big pharma couldn't make billions off it.

And so, the battle lines were clearly drawn.

Hold that horse for a moment—am I seriously advocating for ivermectin as a cancer treatment? No. I'll leave that to the experts (preferably the ones without political agendas). But will I, every now and then, drop the hot potato into casual conversation just to see my oncologist momentarily short-circuit? Absolutely. And if I have to be there, sitting in an expired oatmeal-colored, fluorescent-lit room with all the warmth and charm of an airport security checkpoint, talking about my mutant lung cells, I might as well get a little (actually, a lot of, I must admit) entertainment out of it.

Because while cancer is unpredictable, terrifying and exhausting, there's still one universal truth: Doctors are fun to mess with.

So, if you're ever craving a quick adrenaline rush, just look your oncologist dead in the eye and say, 'Hey doc, what are your thoughts on ivermectin?'

Then sit back and enjoy the show.

CHAPTER 7: BUT FIRST, I HAVE A FEW QUESTIONS...

As I look forward to my next chemo round with all the joy of having a tooth pulled, I decide to kick things up a notch. Sure, I could sit quietly in the infusion chair like a responsible adult, but where's the fun in that? This time, I'm bringing a list of questions. Big, fat, juicy ones. The 'please don't ask this' kind that keep my mother awake at night and make my oncologist blink a little too long. Just because I can.

Here's are my top thirteen questions – more to come:

1. WHY DOES NAUSEA FEEL LIKE IT STARTS IN MY BRAIN?

And follow-up: how do I trick my brain into thinking I'm on a beach in the Maldives instead of Barf City? I'm open to lobotomy-level solutions. And strong cocktail prescriptions.

2. IF I CONCENTRATE REALLY HARD ON ALGEBRA, WILL CHEMO KILL THE CELLS IN MY BRAIN THAT DON'T DO MATH?

If so, I'm fine with this arrangement. They're freeloaders anyway.

3. WOULD DR. BAILEY HAVE MADE IT THROUGH MED SCHOOL WITHOUT YELLING AT EVERYBODY, OR IS THAT A LEGITIMATE COPING MECHANISM I TOO CAN ADOPT FOR CHEMOTHERAPY?

Addendum: is it a tad worrisome that I'm side-tracking your hard-earned medical degree to ask about *Grey's Anatomy?*

4. IS NAUSEA ACTUALLY WORSE THAN PAIN, OR IS THAT JUST A CLEVER BRAIN TRICK TO MAKE ME APPRECIATE PAIN WHEN IT SHOWS UP?

Also, can I complain about both without sounding ungrateful for modern medicine? Because I'd like to.

5. CAN I DONATE MY BRAIN TO SCIENCE AFTER CHEMO, OR IS IT CONSIDERED 'PRE-USED'?

Not that I expect anyone to want it—it's 40 percent sarcasm, 60 percent existential dread and 25 percent useless trivia about animals. The total, you ask? Must be those dying math cells.

6. IF SOMEONE THROWS UP ON A ROLLER COASTER, DOES THE NAUSEA STILL COUNT AS MOTION SICKNESS OR SOMETHING NEW ENTIRELY?

This feels medically benign and worth asking.

7. WHAT'S THE WEIRDEST THING SOMEONE HAS EVER ASKED YOU DURING CHEMO?

Am I now that person?

8. CAN CHEMO MAKE ME TELEPATHIC?

If yes, will I use it responsibly? (Spoiler alert: no.) If no, is there a trial I can sign up for? I'm already here—may as well go all in.

9. DO YOU EVER USE BIG MEDICAL WORDS JUST TO MESS WITH PEOPLE?

Because I would. And I need to know if you're slipping fake Latin into my treatment plan just to see if I'll nod along like a dashboard chicken.

Suggested reply: 'Indubitably, I would not pass up the opportunity. I also need to know if you're slipping some *farrago* into my chemo cocktail just to see if I'll ambulate my neck in acquiescence.'

10. CAN I BLAME CHEMO FOR ANY BAD DECISION-MAKING? LIKE TRAFFIC VIOLATIONS?

Honestly, if it could take the fall for something other than throwing up, I would appreciate that.

11. HAVE YOU EVER PERFORMED A LOBOTOMY?

Not saying I'm volunteering, but I'd like to know what's available if nausea doesn't give me a break this round.

12. IF CHEMO MAKES ME TIRED AND STEROIDS MAKE ME WIRED, WHY DON'T THEY JUST CANCEL EACH OTHER OUT?

Seems like an easy fix. I'd like this one fast-tracked, please.

13. WHAT'S THE SURVIVAL RATE FOR PATIENTS WHO SHOW UP WITH A LIST OF THIRTEEN QUESTIONS?

Asking for a friend.

THE SHIFT

One day, grief didn't yell.
It whispered.
It let me pour my coffee first.
It waited until after I found
my other sock.
And somehow,
that felt like a win.

CHAPTER 8: ON A SCALE OF 1 TO NOPE (DISPATCHES FROM THE MEDICATED FRONTLINES)

Ah, the classic pain scale—that infamous little chart hospitals cling to like it was handed down from the heavens.

'On a scale of 1 to 10, how would you rate your pain?' they ask sweetly, holding a clipboard, their eyes filled with the kind of optimism I haven't felt since 2007.

Let's be honest: pain scales are hilariously subjective. One person stubs a toe and screams for the sweet release of death. Another walks around with a dislocated shoulder and calls it 'a mild inconvenience.' And me? I'm trying to measure my pain while balancing side effects, scanxiety and the deep psychological torment of flavored water. This is not a system built for nuance.

So, for your reading pleasure and my personal satisfaction, I've created a more realistic scale. And tacked a few completely unrelated but highly relevant things I've learned while under the influence of legally sanctioned pharmaceuticals.

THE REVISED PAIN SCALE

1. THE FORGOTTEN MORNING COFFEE

A sharp pang of disappointment. Life is 10 percent less worth living.

Wince Index: 'I'll be dramatic about it, but I'll survive (barely).'

2. THE CRINGE FLASHBACK

That one time you called your teacher Mom. In front of the whole class.

Wince Index: 'I need a blanket, a time machine and maybe a new identity.

3. THE NOT-SO-FUNNY BONE

A jolt of betrayal from your own elbow.

Wince Index: 'Invent new swear words. Blame the furniture.'

4. THE SNEAKY PAPER CUT

Tiny. Treacherous. Suddenly salt is a war crime.

Wince Index: 'Burn the documents. Live ink-free.'

5. THE GOOSE-EYE STANDOFF

No actual injury, just intense psychological warfare with a large bird.

Wince Index: 'I've been judged. And I was found wanting.'

6. THE LEGO MY FOOT-OH

Stepping barefoot on a Lego brick = a rite of passage straight into madness.

Wince Index: 'Reevaluate every decision that led to this moment.'

7. THE LEG CRAMP AT 3 A.M

Mid-dream espionage interrupted by muscle mutiny.

Wince Index: 'And lo, I have been struck down in my sleep.

8. THE SHAKESPEAREAN DEATH SCENE AUDITION

Pinky toe meets furniture. You briefly believe in ghosts.

Wince Index: 'Wherefore art thou, mine quille and caskete fashionéd of crushéd velvette?'

9. THE FULL 'NOPE'

You can't breathe, blink, or form words. You simply are pain.

Wince Index: 'I walk towards a bright light. Say goodbye to my plants.'

Now, add to this mess a solid rotation of cancer medications, fatigue, questionable hospital food and enough paperwork to wallpaper a cathedral. Is it any wonder I find wisdom in the weirdest places?

So, allow me to present...

TEN THINGS
I'VE LEARNED WHILE
MEDICATED

10. DOORKNOBS DESERVE MORE RESPECT

They're loyal. Sturdy. Always within reach. Honestly? Kings of architecture.

9. EVERYTHING IS FUNNIER IN SLOW MOTION

Watching Wes walk across the room feels like ballet. The dogs and I weep with laughter. The cat leaves the room.

8. I MIGHT BE A GENIUS... OR DEEPLY CONFUSED

I once wrote what I thought was the solution to world peace. It was a grocery list. 'More peas' was underlined three times.

7. GRAVITY IS A SUGGESTION

Have you ever thought about walking? Like really thought about it? It's bold. Risky. A leap of faith every single step.

6. BLANKETS HAVE PERSONALITIES

Some hug you. Others attack in your sleep. Sir Snuggles III has my vote for president.

5. FLAVORED WATER IS A SCAM

No lemon, no lime—just lies and disappointment. It tastes like betrayal in liquid form.

4. DAYTIME TV IS A LAWLESS WASTELAND

One moment it's fishing. The next? Competitive llama grooming. I didn't know who I was rooting for, but I was deeply invested.

3. CLOCKS ARE JUDGY

Every tick is a passive-aggressive reminder that you're still horizontal. Mind your business, Clock.

2. HOSPITAL SOCKS DESERVE A HOLIDAY

They're not sexy. But they've saved me from at least three full pratfalls. R.E.S.P.E.C.T.

1. MY PILLOW HAS MOOD SWINGS

Supportive cloud by day. Passive-aggressive brick by night. I now consult it before bedtime.

SO, THE NEXT TIME SOMEONE ASKS HOW I'M FEELING, OR WHAT IT'S LIKE LIVING WITH CHRONIC ILLNESS, I'LL HAND THEM THIS ESSAY. BECAUSE SOMEWHERE BETWEEN THE GOOSE STANDOFFS, THE SINGING DONKEYS ON TV AND THE PILLOW WITH STRONG OPINIONS, THERE'S A TRUTH WORTH LAUGHING AT.

TRUTH IS, IF YOU CAN'T LAUGH WHILE YOUR LEG CRAMPS AT 3 A.M. AND YOUR ONCOLOGIST IS ASKING IF YOU'RE STILL 'REGULAR', WHAT EVEN IS THE POINT?

LAUNDRY
LIST
OF
EMOTION

Monday: hopeful
Tuesday: soggy
Wednesday: rage in a bathrobe
Thursday: medicinally mellow
Friday: I cried over toast
Saturday: hopeful again
Sunday: forecast unclear

CHAPTER 9: THE PILLOW KNOWS

When everything else feels uncertain—when your body's gone rogue, when your energy comes in unpredictable waves, when the hospital has drawn more blood than Dracula—comfort becomes sacred. Not fancy, not dramatic. Just sacred.

A good pillow, fluffed just right, becomes more than cotton and stitching—it becomes control, relief, sanity. The small things, like alignment and softness, start to matter most. Because when your body is at war, peace can be a perfectly fluffed square of fabric under your neck. And on the worst days, that little bit of peace feels like you've won the lottery.

PILLOW FLUFFING FOR MAXIMUM COMFORT 101

Who knew that recovering at home would turn into a crash course in Advanced Pillow Engineering? I mean, at this point, if there were a degree in 'Pillow Placement and Fluffing Science,' I'd be halfway to my master's. I'm trying to train Wes to become my dedicated, on-call, highly trained pillow technician, but he seems to lack interest in the job.

Sometimes it's hard to know what goes on inside other people's heads.

But I digress... I start with what I call 'The Core Four': four pillows, each with a unique purpose. One is for neck support, two for back support and one exists purely on-call and will inevitably be kicked off the bed at 3 a.m. during the leg cramp.

But here's where it gets complicated: the fluff factor. Too fluffy, and I'm bolt upright like a parrot on a perch. Too flat, and I'm sinking like a marshmallow in hot cocoa. It's a delicate balance—one that requires seventeen adjustments per hour, depending on my ever-shifting comfort equilibrium.

Then there's the rotation schedule. Oh yes, I have a system now. Being the devoted pillow-fluffer I am, I rotate each pillow through an elaborate series of flips, smushes and karate-chop fluffing maneuvers. And yes, there is actual technique. Who knew there were so many ways to fluff a pillow? I'm like a conductor performing the 1812 Overture with a very soft orchestra.

All of this to achieve that perfect alignment, which involves coordinating pillows in such a way that they cradle every achy part while leaving enough room for basic survival movements, like breathing.

So, for the ultimate good night's sleep, I encourage you to develop your pillow-fluffing prowess. You could be one fluff away from making it into the Pillow (Fluffery?) Hall of Fame, which I imagine involves a lot of very cool pillows.

And to all those struggling to master this sacred art: keep fluffing on. May your pillows rise to meet you, and may your fluffing hand never tire.

'Into each life some rain must fall.'

— Henry Wadsworth Longfellow,
The Rainy Day

PART

THREE:

Some people inherit wealth. Some inherit land, jewelry or really great cheekbones.

Me? I inherited a cast of characters. Loud ones. Complicated ones. The kind who bring you a casserole, curse your name under their breath and hug so hard they rearrange your ribcage.

They are many things: generous, dramatic, loyal, unpredictable. And somehow, they're all mine.

These essays dive headfirst into the chaos I come from. The people I love. The people I try to understand. The ones who made me who I am—for better or worse, usually both before breakfast.

INHERITED CHAOS

Here you'll meet my family: the dramatic, the delightful, the ones who argue over gravy and hug like it's a full-contact sport. And my Amish friends, who are no less wild in their own quiet, fiercely faithful way. Keepers of tradition, wisdom and the occasional surprise goat.

These stories are tender and tangled. They're about the ache of loving people you can't always help. The comedy of trying to break generational habits while accidentally becoming them. And the strange, beautiful comfort of knowing you come from a line of people who love you in their own broken and brilliant way.

CHAPTER 10: LOVE WITHOUT A MAP

I remember it like it was yesterday.

My son was the first grandchild on both sides. My pregnancy was highly anticipated, heralded by friends and family, celebrated with showers, wrapped in expectation and draped in the kind of excitement that only a firstborn can bring. He was loved before he ever took his first breath.

And when he arrived, he was perfect. The most beautiful child. Angelic. A porcelain-skinned masterpiece. He had the kind of face that stopped strangers. He was gentle and bright, quick to smile, eager to learn. He thrived in love and flourished in attention.

My relationship with his father had been strained from the start. Two young people trying to build something on an already cracked foundation. By the time he was four, he had two younger siblings, both equally loved, equally adored, and a divorce that was inevitable. The next several years played out in custody agreements and court orders. A life scheduled by work shifts rather than the actual needs of the children.

It was sloppy, complicated, sometimes outright incoherent. It was a mess.

But there was always love.

Through the uncertainty, there were birthday parties, every single year. Extravagant Christmases where the tree was drowning in presents, limbs sagging from the weight of our attempts to soften the blows of a divided home. There were vacations, school programs, family gatherings where the laughter swelled so high it threatened to burst through the walls.

I remarried, and my new husband, twelve years my senior, took on the challenge of my young family with a grace that felt like a gift. He loved my children immediately. Fully. Without hesitation. And they loved him back.

And then came the day.

It was nothing remarkable, at least on the surface. We were in the kitchen. I asked him to put something away. I don't remember what. A dish? A book? Something so small it shouldn't have even warranted a second thought.

He looked me straight in the eye and said, 'No.'

And that was it. The beginning of the unraveling. The first fissure in the foundation.

I don't know if I could have recognized it then, but now I see it for what it was—a shift, a break, a door slamming shut on the child I had known. From that moment on, he became someone else. Like some dramatic cinematic transformation. Slowly, steadily, he withdrew like the tide eroding the shore until the landscape was unrecognizable.

What followed was a descent into a world I never knew existed. The next ten years became a living hell. We dove headfirst into the behavioral health system—a wretched, broken labyrinth of hollow

promises and Band-Aid solutions. Every door led to another hallway of uncertainty. Every answer only led to more questions. There were therapies that didn't work. Treatment plans that dissolved before they could begin. Diagnoses that felt more like labels than solutions.

It was a blur of institutionalizations, temporary stabilizations, and therapists who were as lost as we were. The behavioral programs felt more like prison sentences. At one point, he ended up in what I can only describe as a crack house disguised as therapy. A facility that promised structure and healing but delivered chaos and more trauma.

Nothing worked.

Nothing.

And we tried everything.

There's plenty of blame to go around. Regrets that burn holes in my soul.

He quit school. He ran. He fell into drugs. He disappeared into a world that swallowed him whole. He was homeless at times. He was angry. So angry. At us. At the world. At himself.

And yet, we never stopped loving him.

To this day, he lives in the shadows. A ghost of the boy I once cradled. He scrapes by, barely existing, clinging to the edge of survival. He has a child of his own now. Tangled in a harrowing relationship that is its own tragedy, playing out on a stage we can no longer reach.

I wish I could tell you there was a happy ending. That he came back to us. That he healed. That I woke up one morning to the sound of his laughter drifting through the house. That same laugh that used to bubble up from deep in his belly and spill into every room like sunlight.

But I can't.

What I can tell you is that I mourn him every day.

I mourn the child he was. The man he could have been.

We all do.

And maybe that is the cruelest part of love—the fact that it never stops, even when the person you love is no longer reachable. Even when they are lost in a way that feels irreversible.

We suffer the arrows of condemnation. The whispered accusations of what we did to him. Whether intentional or not.

We   did   the   best   we   could.

We   fought   for   him.   We   sacrificed   for   him.

We   tried   to   save   him   from

himself.   Where   did   we   go   wrong?   The

questions   are   endless.   The   guilt   is   bottomless.

The   love   is   unshakable.

'The only noise now was the rain, pattering softly with the magnificent indifference of nature for the tangled passions of humans.'

— Sherwood Smith

AFTERMATH

I thought I was the storm.
Turns out I was the field—
bent, soaked, bruised...
and still growing.

CHAPTER 11: MEET MY DAD (THE LEGEND, THE GRUMP, THE SHARK WHISPERER)

My dad. A devilishly handsome guy of Sicilian descent, with more quirks than a vintage cuckoo clock. He dressed like he was about to step into a Hollywood leading role—clothes always impeccably pressed, not a wrinkle in sight, shoes polished to a mirror shine, and jet-black hair slicked back in perfect defiance of gravity. He could charm the socks right off you, but linger too long in his way and he'd have no problem telling you where to go and how to get there. Fast.

My dad's laugh was a masterpiece of hilarity—part snicker, part wheeze and entirely contagious. It wasn't the kind that demanded attention, like an asthmatic trying to catch their breath. Think Muttley, the wheezy cartoon dog, but with more charm and less fur. When he got going, it was impossible not to join in, even if you didn't know what was so funny. His laugh had this magical way of turning the most ordinary moments into side-splitting comedy.

It was the sound of pure mischief, and hearing it felt like being let in on the world's funniest secret.

One of his quirks was his total intolerance for minor inconveniences. A squeaky door? He'd slam it like he was fighting a wild animal. A drippy faucet? You'd think it was an oil rig disaster. And breathing too loudly? That was apparently a personal attack on his peace. Somehow, any small irritation or worse, a combination, would send him over the edge. And it was hilarious to watch.

Dad had this ability to convince us kids of the most absurd things, mostly for his own entertainment. Case in point: he once swore there were sharks in the lake where we vacationed. Not just any sharks—hungry, child-eating sharks. We didn't swim for three summers. Some of us never swam again. He laughed every time he saw us tippy-toeing ankle-deep, scanning for fins.

He had a gambler's heart and the luck of a broken mirror. Every family game night was a masterclass in barely legal cheating. 'I didn't cheat, I'm just smarter than you,' he'd say, while blatantly tucking an extra Queen of Hearts up his sleeve. Don't even get me started on Monopoly—he always owned Boardwalk, but none of us ever saw him buy it.

Despite all his antics, our childhood friends adored him. He gave everyone ridiculous nicknames like Pigface, Flyface, Dogface, Bolognaface, Chairface—whatever popped into his head. We howled with laughter, but somehow it never felt mean. That was just how he loved people—loudly, weirdly, completely.

As the firstborn, I reveled in my status. Spoiled, pampered and convinced I was royalty. I had a scream that could shatter glass.

High-pitched, long-lasting, the kind that could summon rescue helicopters. And I used it. Often. Whether my cracker broke in two or I got a boo-boo, the whole household had to know. I was a drama queen with the clumsiness of a cartoon character. I tripped, fell, bruised and bled like it was my job.

My dad didn't find it quite as entertaining. If I scraped my knee or tumbled down the stairs (don't ask, it's a skill), he'd lose it. One time he declared I was never allowed near stairs again. At 17, I also got Super Glue banned. Permanently.

He loved me, no question. But let's be honest—he was happiest when I wasn't actively driving him crazy. Looking back, I probably drained him of every ounce of energy. If things were quiet, that was a win. But one phrase echoed through my childhood and teenage years. During one of his wild-eyed rants, he'd say it like a curse: 'When you grow up, I hope you have a daughter JUST LIKE yourself, and I'm going to laugh!'

At the time, I'd roll my eyes. *Whatever, Dad.* But it wasn't just a throwaway line. It was his revenge strategy. And I now realize how hilarious—and terrifying—those words were, when they eventually came to pass.

On a cold winter day in January, I welcomed a daughter into the world. A little pink bundle of joy wrapped in a blanket of karma. My dad's wish had come true. She was, in every way, exactly like me. From the moment she could toddle, she mastered drama. A cracked cookie? Tragedy. A misplaced stuffed animal? Full-scale manhunt. And when the seam of her sock didn't sit just right? Oh, the wailing

could summon neighbors from three blocks away.

Her scream? Identical to mine. Pierced walls, rattled windows, sent the dog under the bed. I could practically hear my dad snickering from the great beyond, loving every second of it. She was clumsy, just like me. Constantly falling off chairs, tripping over nothing, finding every sharp edge in the house. And yes, I reacted the same way my dad did—wild-eyed and panicked, swearing she'd never climb a tree again or leave the couch ever.

Then came the theatrics. One stubbed toe and she'd be flat out in the living room, demanding ice packs, a foot rub and maybe a will to be drawn up, 'just in case.' I'd find her echoing my wild-eyed saying: 'Somebody bring me an ice pick so I can stab myself in the head!' But it wasn't just the antics. It was the energy. She threw herself into life with the same exhausting flair I once had. She drained me. And yet, I couldn't stop marveling at her. She was my mini-me, my mirror, my karmic payback.

And like my dad, I loved her to pieces. It's funny how genetics work, isn't it? They say we pass on more than eye color and curly hair. Apparently, my DNA was feeling extra. It passed on my entire essence.

I imagine the production meeting when my cells got together to craft her blueprint:

Cell 1: 'We're giving her The Scream, right?'

Cell 2: 'Absolutely. Let's crank it up an octave. Dogs need to hear it too.'

Cell 3: 'What about the drama?'

Cell 2: 'Oh, 100 percent.'

Cell 4: 'Teenage angst?'

Cell 2: 'Let's extend that into adulthood this time.'

Because apparently, every cell in my body had a memory. And not only did they remember me—they focused on my most distinct qualities and gift-wrapped them for the next generation. How thoughtful. It's almost poetic. Like my DNA heard my dad's wish and said, 'We can make that happen.' And somewhere, my dad is snickering.

So now, I'm caught in the ultimate genetic loop. Every time my daughter flings herself on the couch in despair or wails about starving to death because there's 'NEVER anything to eat in this house,' I think of my Dad and say to myself, 'Well, Dad, you got your wish!' And just because I can, I keep the tradition alive. I look her straight in the eye, channel my dad's exasperated energy and say, 'Someday, I hope you have a daughter exactly like you. And you know what? I'm gonna laugh.'

Because that's the beauty of genetics. Of karma. Of the circle of life. It all comes back around.

With an elephant's memory and a headache the size of New Jersey.

CHAPTER 12: THE WOMEN WHO RAISED ME (AND EACH OTHER)

Also known as The King Sisters, the Eye-Rollers, and the Ones Who Taught Me That Lipstick Is Not Optional

If I had to describe the women in my family, I'd say this: they are funny, fiercely loyal and always, always, well-groomed. They could burn a roast, forget a birthday and still show up with perfect hair and a lipstick shade that matched their handbag. These women made excellent moms, but somehow, even better grandmas. Probably because by that point, they'd stopped trying to control everything and just started laughing at it instead.

On my mother's side, there were four sisters—sharp, stylish, tight-knit and endlessly entertaining. My uncle always called them The King Sisters, which I assumed was either a reference to a vintage singing group or some elite girl gang that held their meetings in the church basement over coffee and cake. I never got a clear answer. I just knew the name fit. They were glamorous in a very approachable way—like they'd fix your hemline while telling a mildly inappropriate joke—and they loved each other with a loyalty so seamless it practically had choreography.

On my dad's side were his two older sisters: beautiful, bold, and as Italian as a triple shot of espresso on a Sunday morning. Their love language was sarcasm. Their spiritual gift was the dramatic eye roll. Being around them was like being dropped into a live-action Sicilian variety show—equal parts laughter, unsolicited advice and pasta. If you weren't laughing, you were probably being roasted.

Somehow, from all of this estrogen and eyeliner, came me.

We all tried, at one point or another, not to become one another. We'd say things like, 'Well, *I* won't say things like that to *my* kids' or 'Just because *she* does that doesn't mean I will.' And yet here I am—quick with a laugh, deeply attached to my Oil of Olay, and genetically incapable of keeping my opinion to myself.

These next stories are about the women I come from. The ones who shaped me, spoiled me, humbled me and handed me their best advice, both unasked for and emotionally charged. We were loud. We were close. We were quick with a joke, fast with a hug and dangerously over-invested in each other's business.

And honestly? I wouldn't trade a single eye-roll for anything.

CHAPTER 13: WHAT COLOR WAS NANA'S HAIR REALLY?

Was it gray?

Silver?

Lavender?

Or did she just roll her curls in a bowl of fresh-cut lilacs because it made her feel fancy? Was that a thing back then? A status symbol? 'Look at my hair, I've ascended to lavender.'

I never asked.

There are a lot of things I never asked Nana.

Like why she always wore those oversized, boxy button-down apron-things she called housecoats. Were they coats? Were they for the house? Were they for house combat? Because they were made of the sturdiest floral fabric known to mankind, and she wore them like armor. Always with two giant pockets stuffed with tissues, rosary beads and the occasional hard butterscotch candy wrapped in a crinkly yellow wrapper that looked like it had lived there since Nixon was President.

And speaking of the candies—why butterscotch? Was there a national grandmother agreement? Was there a time when Werther's Originals were sold door-to-door and they all bought them in bulk?

I don't know. But I do know that walking into Nana and Nanu's house on a Sunday was like stepping into another universe—a basil-and-mint-scented universe where garlic had its own gravitational pull and meatballs floated through the air on tiny clouds of tomato sauce.

Nana's cooking wasn't just good—it was *legendary*. I've never tasted anything like it—ever.

Her sauce simmered for hours. Her meatballs were wrapped in breadcrumbs and love (and probably a little guilt.)

Was there cinnamon in the sauce? Or nutmeg?

Why was it sweet and perfect and magical?

Why didn't I ask for the recipe?

WHY didn't ANYONE ask for the recipe?

Because we were too busy eating. And yelling.

Sunday dinners always started with such promise. The table was full, everyone was laughing, Nana was stirring and beaming and occasionally throwing her hands in the air for reasons unknown. The sauce was rich, the bread was warm and then—boom—someone gave someone else a side-eye.

That was all it took.

Suddenly, voices were raised. Hands were flying. Accusations were launched in rapid-fire. I didn't know exactly what was being said (because it was in Italian), but judging by the hand flailing and occasional dish slamming, I knew it wasn't 'pass the salad.'

That's it! Everybody OUT!'

And then, just like that, the evening was over.

Thrown out. Again. A family tradition.

I never knew whether we were going for dinner or a live re-enactment of an opera about betrayal and overcooked pasta.

And let's not forget the remote control. Nana never used it. She feared it. She'd hold it like a cursed object, pointing it at the TV with suspicion, like at any moment it might blow up the entire living room or open a portal to somewhere worse (like a channel showing kissing).

She'd just hold it... then get up to change the channel by hand.

Nana loved a good guilt trip. *Why don't you come visit more?* she'd ask, the way other people ask *Why don't you care about my soul?*

The tone was similar.

She wore her hairnets like they were crowns. She wore slippers like they were designer heels. She cursed with the elegance of a mafia don and hugged like her arms were made of dough and cinnamon.

She was magic.

Messy, dramatic, purple-haired, sauce-slinging magic.

And if I close my eyes, I can still smell her kitchen. Still feel the heat from the oven. Still hear the arguments stirring up in the other room.

Still see Nana, standing at the stove in her floral housecoat, ladle in hand, ready for battle.

Now, somebody pass the meatballs before things get loud.

'Be like water,
Flow like a river,
Crash like the rain,
Fly like the cloud
again!'

— Md. Ziaul Haque

CHAPTER 14: LIPSTICK & LIES

'Never trust a woman not wearing any lipstick.'

That was my grandmother's cardinal rule, the hill she chose to die on, the single unshakable belief that guided her through life as she confidently navigated the cosmetics aisle at The Bon Ton. She never explained it—never sat me down and said, 'Here's why, dear.' No, it was just understood, absorbed through osmosis, passed down like a sacred Revlon scroll.

The women in my family all carried lipstick like a secret weapon, a hidden lie detector tucked neatly into the darkest corners of our purses. It wasn't for vanity. It wasn't even for beauty. It was for something deeper, something primal. Bright pink or red lipstick marks were as much a part of my childhood as Wrigley's Gum, the Schwanny guy and the smell of Aqua Net permanently affixed to the bathroom walls.

But why?

Why did my grandma believe that the bare-lipped were fundamentally untrustworthy? Did she think a woman who couldn't commit to lipstick couldn't commit to anything? Did she have a traumatic experience with a chapstick-wielding con artist? Had she been tricked out of an estate inheritance by a suspiciously pale-mouthed cousin? Had a lipstick-less best friend borrowed her

Tupperware and hasn't returned it yet?

And what did it mean when she encountered someone with only lip liner? Was that woman on the verge of a breakdown? A liar of the highest order? Or simply running late?

What about the woman who used lipstick but applied it with reckless abandon, veering outside the lines of her lips like a toddler with a red Sharpie in a white room? Was she to be pitied? Feared? Reported to the authorities?

I never asked. Because you don't ask. You just listened, nod solemnly and reapply frequently, like a responsible person.

My grandma, of course, never left the house without looking like she'd stepped straight out of an Estée Lauder ad. Her lips were always perfectly painted, lined and sealed for longevity, as if she were preparing for an impromptu meeting with the Pope or a last-minute invitation to dine with the Queen. I don't think I ever saw her apply lipstick. It was always just there. Like a part of her face, more permanent than her own fingerprints.

It occurs to me now that she probably did trust a woman without lipstick. Just not with anything important. You could probably borrow a cup of sugar from her with bare lips, maybe even a casserole dish, but a family secret? A bank deposit? Absolutely not.

And this is where it all falls apart.

Because—God help me—I don't wear lipstick.

Not even for special occasions. Not even for funerals (which would send my grandmother rolling in her perfectly powdered grave). My whole generation abandoned the Lipstick Code entirely.

Somewhere along the way, we swapped Revlon Red for Burt's Bees and settled in with a false sense of confidence.

What would Grandma think if she saw us now, walking around in broad daylight, our lips naked and vulnerable to the world? Would she tut-tut in disappointment? Would she pull me aside and whisper, 'Honey, I love you, but you are not to be trusted.'

I don't know.

Still, when I picture her in my mind—lips perfectly painted, raising an eyebrow at my (gasp!) underdressed mouth—I can't help but think... she'd probably have a point.

And with that thought, I reach into my purse, past the loose gum wrappers and emergency dog treats, and sigh.

Grandma may be gone, but I can still hear her, clear as day: 'For heaven's sake Christy, put some color on those lips before people start asking questions.'

'This is what fun is like,' said Rain, almost to herself.

— Gregory Maguire, *Out of Oz*

CHAPTER 15: THE WIND BENEATH MY RADIO CAREER

It was one of those painfully perfect spring days. You know the kind—birds harmonizing like Disney extras, sunshine spotlighting every dust particle with judgmental clarity, and a breeze so gentle it felt like Mother Nature whispering, *'Don't mess this up.'* My mom, my 18-year-old niece Hannah, and I were all sitting outside, enjoying the type of weather that makes you believe life isn't, in fact, a tragic comedy.

Hannah had just gotten accepted to the University of Buffalo, because apparently, she's smart, focused and not genetically burdened by the kind of decision-making skills that once led me to ruin a perfectly good GPA in under a semester. College talk was in the air, floating around like pollen and I could feel my lungs tightening, not from allergies, but from the incoming embarrassment.

Hannah mentioned a girl she knew—one of those free-spirited freshmen who treated her first year of college like a music festival with a tuition bill. 'She's just out partying every night,' Hannah said, 'failing everything, and her parents have no idea.'

This, my friends, is the moment the barometric pressure dropped in my soul. I felt the storm coming the way you feel a suspicious wetness in your sock five minutes into a hike—ominous, inescapable and definitely about to ruin something.

My mind tried to tiptoe away from the conversation like a cartoon mouse trying to sneak away with a treat. Tippy toe... tippy toe...

'Stop,' my mother said.

She didn't yell. She didn't even raise her voice. But she might as well have pulled a fire alarm in my chest.

She turned to Hannah with the sugar-sweet tone that always precedes a full-blown character assassination cloaked in maternal pride.

'Do you know who else did that their first year of college?'

Red alert. Red alert. We have a breach. Sirens in my brain. My inner monologue was sprinting in all directions. My soul was trying to fake an injury to get out of the room.

I froze like a possum caught mid-crime in someone's garage.

Then she looked at me, *smiling*. Always beware the smiling.

'Help me remember, Christina,' she said. 'Was it a carnival you joined or a motorcycle gang?'

'It was a radio station, Mom.'

'Oh, that's right,' she said, her face lighting up with the satisfaction of storytelling and public humiliation. 'You were going to be a disc jockey!'

'A journalist,' I whispered, clinging to that last syllable like a lifeline. A tiny, crumpled shred of dignity flapping in the breeze of her unraveling monologue.

I knew it. The whole thing was coming out. There would be no mercy. This tale was now a teaching moment, and teaching moments in my family come with sequels, commentary and dramatic reenactments.

'It was a noble profession,' I defended, clinging to the narrative like it was a flotation device in a sea of poor choices. 'Plus, I met my boyfriend there. And I ran weekend hockey games.'

Clearly, my soggy attempts at embellishment weren't waterproof. They were leaking from all sides.

My mom squinted, deep in thought. You could see the memory reel whirring in her brain. 'How did we find out again? Do you remember?'

I tried to disappear into my chair. 'Someone... may have heard me on the radio... and told you,' I mumbled.

I wanted Hannah to know I wasn't a complete derelict. I had intentions. Beautiful, vague intentions. 'I was planning on going back to class. Just not during hockey season.'

Mom's tone turned sing-songy again—never a good sign. 'And then,' she continued with dramatic flair, 'she couldn't understand why we wouldn't pay for her to go to travel school to become an airline stewardess two years later.'

I sighed. 'Probably not my best debate performance.'

Hannah laughed in disbelief, the kind of laugh that says, *my aunt was a full-blown sitcom character and somehow survived into adulthood.* She looked at me like I had just told her I once auditioned for Cirque du Soleil without stretching first.

'I don't even know why I wanted to be a stewardess,' I admitted.

'I didn't even like people.'

To recap: dropped out of college, took up residence at a radio station, fell in love with a news reporter who smelled of coffee and youthful rebellion, declared my new dream of becoming airborne in heels and polyester, and somehow thought this résumé would sway my parents to invest more in my educational whiplash.

'Honestly, I still don't know why the travel school thing didn't work out. I would have looked great in that scarf,' I announced.

But there, on that perfect spring day, under a sun that was far too bright for the amount of shame I was absorbing, I realized something. These stories—these wild, cringey, delightfully disastrous chapters—weren't just embarrassing. They were proof. Proof that I had once been young, dumb and full of misguided ambition.

And if you've never dreamed of being a journalist/DJ/hockey announcer/flight attendant while simultaneously skipping class and inventing new ways to disappoint your parents, have you even really *lived*?

CHAPTER 16: GREAT EXPECTATIONS (AND OTHER CHRONIC CONDITIONS)

I have a disease.

No, not cancer—although yes, unfortunately, I have that too. No, I'm talking about something far more insidious. More persistent. More soul-crushing. It's called Setting My Expectations to Idyllic and Failing Miserably Every Single Time Syndrome (SMEIFMESTS).

It's genetic. I get it from my mother.

She is the original carrier of the mutation—the one who plans the perfect holiday like it's a Norman Rockwell painting, only to end the night whispering in the kitchen, 'Next year, I'm inviting strangers. At least they pretend to behave.'

Ironically, I spend a fair amount of time coaching her on this very topic:

'Mom, lower your expectations. Remember who's coming. It's your family, not a Hallmark movie cast. Prepare for chaos. Possibly bloodshed.'

And then I'll turn around and build my own tower of intentions with the wild-eyed excitement of someone who's never been burned—booking reservations, sending cheerful invites, fluffing my expectations—only to end up wondering why humans, myself included, continue to climb the rickety ladder of hope like we've never fallen off it before.

Why can't my simple, overachieving brain learn? I'm 56. I've had enough failed expectations to earn an honorary doctorate in Disappointment Studies. And still, I show up to life like a chihuahua at a surprise party, convinced this time will be different. This time, people will behave. Events will go smoothly. Nothing will explode.

It's like trying to eat just one bowl of cereal.

It simply.

Cannot.

Be done.

Luckily for me, I am incredibly resilient. Like, absurdly so. When the house of expectations collapses (again), all I need is a minimum three-hour nap and bingo! I'm back. Refreshed. Renewed. Perched like a wide-eyed optimist on the edge of the next train track.

Now... naps.

Oh, how I love them. I crave naps the way nanas crave plastic couch covers and Werther's Originals.

But naps, glorious, sacred naps.

There are rules, of course.

· Too short, and I wake up like a bear who's been yanked from hibernation to find it's still snowing in April.

· Too long, and I simply cancel the rest of the day and extend the whole thing into a full night's sleep. Because why not?

· The perfect nap is somewhere between deep REM cycle and light coma, ideally with a weighted blanket and no responsibilities for 2–4 hours post-wake.

But I digress.

The real point is this:

I am a chronically hopeful human, trapped in a reality where things rarely go according to plan.

And maybe that's not entirely a bad thing. Because even though my expectations often set me up for disappointment, they also mean I'm still out here, trying. Hoping. Setting the table for magic, even if I know trauma is more likely to be served up.

And when the whole thing inevitably explodes into a glittery disaster of unmet dreams and dropped casseroles, I'll just take a nap, adjust my tiara and start all over again.

CHAPTER 17: A LOWCOUNTRY HOOTENANNY (ONE MARINE, TWO MATRIARCHS AND A WOMAN WITH SWOLLEN FEET)

I made the bold, impulsive decision to take my mother and her sister, my Aunt Janet, on a trip to visit my son in Charleston, South Carolina—a city known for its charm, its heat and as I would soon discover, its alarming number of cobblestone streets (which are apparently designed to test both balance and podiatry).

My son, freshly done with a five-year tour in the Marines, had chosen to settle there—a place where the streets whisper history, the food scene could bankrupt a Rockefeller, and the rent requires either a side hustle or a small inheritance. He is a structured, no-nonsense type with champagne taste, and a kitchen fully stocked with cutting-edge gadgets that no one is allowed to touch. He greeted us like a man who had read the itinerary, prepared the house and knew full well that the women arriving were a walking hurricane of thrift, volume and uncalled for opinions.

First up: my mother. Nana is what we lovingly call her. She's a serial worrier, thrift store connoisseur, and a human information kiosk who has never, in her entire life, not asked someone for directions—even when she's holding a GPS, a printed MapQuest page and a compass. She insists on triple-confirming every restaurant's location, parking situation and bathroom proximity like we're planning a lunar landing.

Aunt Janet, on the other hand, floats through life on a pastel cloud of okie-dokies and quiet contentment. She is what would happen if a lavender cardigan came to life and discovered T.J. Maxx. She shops with the reckless abandon of someone who believes God created discounts for her specifically. Once, she tried to buy a decorative bowl from a bar and grill, mistaking it for a charming boutique display.

And then there's me. Human behavior observer. Professional eye-roller. The one with zero patience, two perpetually swollen feet, and the unenviable job of wrangling this multi-generational tornado through a weekend getaway in the South. Trying to reach a group consensus with this crew is like herding geckos across a hot skillet. One minute we're on our way to brunch, the next we're pulled into a church thrift sale because Nana spotted a sign for Gently Worn Purses.

Charleston itself didn't stand a chance.

We went to the Charleston City Market, where my mother audibly gasped at the historic architecture, clutching her fanny pack like it contained national secrets and asking complete strangers if they happened to know what that particular style of wrought iron was called (spoiler: they did not). Aunt Janet got swallowed whole by the sea of vendors—last seen drifting somewhere between the sweetgrass baskets and the gourmet jams—while I nearly got taken out by a tour bus because I was too busy admiring a horse-drawn carriage.

Meanwhile, my son stood silently nearby, arms crossed, watching us with the exhausted patience of a man found this outing more emotionally taxing than crawling through mud with a 70-pound pack.

One night, after a long day of navigating uneven sidewalks and unwelcome architectural facts, we decided to wind down with a movie. My son, ever the cultured one with lofty taste, suggested we watch *Dune*. You know, the epic sci-fi saga that requires a minor in political science, a PhD in intergalactic warfare and the attention span of a monk.

Let me tell you—*we were not ready*.

Ten minutes in, Nana had already asked if we could pause the movie to 'just quickly go over who that man in the robe was and what his problem seemed to be.'

We paused for snacks.

We paused for volume adjustments.

We paused so Nana could go to the bathroom.

We paused because I needed a drink and couldn't figure out how the microwave worked ('It keeps saying PRESS START but nothing's starting.)

And then there was the dog. My son's Samoyed—a majestic, 75-pound cloud with boundary issues—decided the best place to watch *Dune* was directly on my shins. As my feet swelled like two unwilling balloons, this furry avalanche sighed contentedly and refused to budge. Every time we shifted her off, she clambered right back up with all the urgency of a toddler who smelled cookies.

By the end of the movie, we had no idea who the villain was, what the plot involved or why there was so much sand. But we did know this: Nana thinks the whole thing was a biblical parable, and that 'sand is very spiritual.'

Honestly, *Dune* didn't stand a chance either.

And yet—it was perfect.

Because somehow, in the middle of the chaos, we laughed so hard. We made memories I'll cherish until I'm 94 and cranky in a recliner. Watching my son beam with pride as he gave us a tour of his new life was worth every throbbing toe and detour through a consignment shop.

Plus, Nana got a new purse, a handwritten map from a stranger and a refrigerator magnet that says 'Bless Your Heart.' Aunt Janet got two hundred pamphlets, ten light spring sweaters, two skirts and three fridge magnets. And me? I got a full page of notes, a deeper appreciation for compression socks, and a reminder that family is always a wild, wonderful circus—and I'm lucky enough to hold a front-row seat.

'There is no more beautiful love story than that between wind and rain.'

— Corina Abdulahm Negura

CHAPTER 18: WES, MY FOREVER STEADY

Some people marry their soulmate. I somehow managed to marry my soul's *anchor*. My husband Wes is the most wonderful man I could've ever dreamed up... and trust me, I have a very vivid imagination.

He is quiet, calm and strong in that deeply rooted way that doesn't announce itself, but you feel it. He has a heart so golden it could be studied by alchemists. And during my cancer journey, he's been a rock. No, scratch that. A fortress. The kind you could build a whole kingdom around.

While I'm out here living life as part firecracker, part Road Runner, part Whack-a-Mole—pinging from one idea to the next like a hungry squirrel—Wes is the keel. The quiet, steady force that keeps me upright when the waters rise. Without him, I'd be a weather balloon with a hole in it, spinning wildly over rural Pennsylvania and getting tangled in someone's wind chimes.

What makes Wes even more lovable, if that's possible, is his joyful disposition. He's just genuinely happy. Not in a performative way. In the dependable, loving, Golden Retriever way. Willing to carry the heavy stuff without ever asking for credit.

Which brings me to Tennessee. And the time I absolutely lost it on my honeymoon.

Now, I hate being lost. I mean, truly, deeply despise it. Not just on the

road, but in life. Since my cancer diagnosis, I've felt that disorientation more than ever—the sense of being dropped into a foreign place with no signage, no compass and absolutely no map. And while I'm doing my best to navigate this strange terrain with humor and grace, the truth is, I've always had a complicated relationship with uncertainty. I like direction. I like clear routes. I like knowing where I'm going and how long it'll take to get there, with snacks packed and bathroom breaks pre-planned. Wandering aimlessly—physically or emotionally—short-circuits my brain. It's not just aggravation; a sheer, visceral panic sets in. It's as though the entire universe mocks me. My brain doesn't interpret being lost as a minor hiccup; it sees it as a full-blown existential crisis.

My husband, Wes, discovered this about me the hard way—on our honeymoon.

The plan was simple: take a long, rambling drive from western Pennsylvania to Louisiana, enjoying the open road and all its charming detours. For a while, everything was smooth sailing. We cruised through state after state, laughing, talking, and basking in the glow of newlywed bliss. That is, until we hit Tennessee.

Somewhere in the middle of the very large Volunteer State, I started to feel uneasy. You know that creeping sensation, like a storm cloud gathering on the horizon? I couldn't shake the feeling that we were driving due west—or worse, north. Don't ask me why; it's not like I had any frame of reference, because logically, our atlas was buried in the trunk.

I tried to stay calm, but the knot in my stomach wou'dn't budge.

'Honey,' I said, with the forced casualness of a person teetering on the edge of a meltdown, 'maybe we should stop at a gas station to grab a Tennessee map.'

Wes, of course, had no such sense of impending doom. He was merrily tapping the steering wheel to a tune only he could hear, completely at peace within his universe.

In moments like this, Wes is the human version of a golden retriever—relaxed, easy-going and perpetually happy. Even if we were hopelessly lost, he'd approach the situation like a retriever in a new park, sniffing around, wagging his tail and eventually wandering off in a new direction. No map? No problem. The journey itself was the adventure. Minor details, like knowing where we were, were just part of the fun.

Meanwhile, I was internally combusting.

'Wes,' I said, my voice deepening, 'We. Are. Lost.'

'We're not lost,' he said, like I'd just suggested we buy beachfront property in Malibu. 'I know exactly where I am.'

Snap.

'You do not know where we are!' I declared, waving toward the Tennessee darkness. 'You've never been here before! You don't know where you're going! It's the middle of the night! You're driving blindfolded!'

Wes, to his credit, said nothing. He just watched me unravel, and wondered what kind of lunatic he'd married.

After what felt like an eternity, we finally pulled into a dimly-lit gas station to unearth the atlas. Sure enough, we'd taken a wrong turn about 50 miles back.

The ride back to the right road was... silent. Not the peaceful, companionable kind, but the kind of silence that hums with warning.

By the time we hit Georgia, my madness had ebbed. The absurdity of it all sank in, and we started laughing.

Looking back, that moment was a defining one in our marriage. It set the tone for all the times we'd veer off course—literally or figuratively—and find our way back together, laughing at the ridiculousness of it all.

Sure, I lost it in Tennessee... but I also found a man who stayed calm, stayed kind and stayed married to me. I think that earns him a lifetime subscription.

'Kiss me with rain on your eyelashes, come on, let us sway together, under the trees, and to hell with thunder.'

— Edwin Morgan, *A Book of Lives*

CHAPTER 19: BEFORE YOU TURN THE PAGE

Some stories are easier to tell than others. They come with punchlines and perspective and just enough distance to soften the blow. But then there are the ones that still sting when you say them out loud. The ones you carry like a stone in your pocket, worn smooth over time but never quite gone.

These next few stories come from that place.

They're about the harder moments. The ones shaped by grief, estrangement, mental illness and the aching, complicated kind of love that doesn't always wrap itself in neat endings. These pieces aren't dressed up in humor. They aren't tidy or polished. They're just honest. And telling them was both painful and necessary.

If you've ever carried your own heaviness, your own version of a wound that still pulses when the weather changes, then I hope you'll find something here that makes you feel less alone. That maybe these stories, in all their mess and truth, help light a path through your own.

And don't worry, I eventually go back to being ridiculous. Just after these few pages.

A MERRY AND MESSY CHRISTMAS

I woke up on the couch. Much to my disappointment. Drenched in sweat, mildly nauseous, with a pounding headache—the usual suspects of my 'new normal,' courtesy of chemo.

Two cold, wet noses nudged me into reality. Tucker and Maggie, my ever-faithful four-legged companions, tails wagging furiously and panting like living metronomes, hovered like cheerful little nurses with no credentials but boundless enthusiasm. Clearly, my stillness on the couch had been noted in their canine blogs as a delay in their sacred 5:30 a.m. ritual: the Great Backyard Inspection.

'Okay, okay,' I croaked, waving them off like a hungover queen addressing her royal subjects. But their joy didn't waver. Dogs have this miraculous ability to turn even your most bedraggled moments into a reason for celebration.

I stood quietly, leaning on the doorframe as the two explorers set off into the pre-dawn world. Maggie, my 14-year-old elder stateswoman, moved with the careful deliberation of someone who had earned the right to take her sweet time. Her trusty nose led the way, as if she were piecing together the mysteries of life, one whiff at a time. Tucker, on the other hand, was pure chaos—bouncing and leaping like Tigger fresh out of A.A. Milne's wood.

I smiled as he launched himself into the air after some invisible foe, possibly a snowflake, possibly his own shadow. It was a performance equal parts graceful and ridiculous, a kinetic blur of goldendoodle energy.

The sweetest sight of all, though, was Tucker's pause from his joyful escapades to tend to Maggie. With the care of a devoted healer, he licked the countless cancer sores scattered across her frail body—an act of pure instinct, pure love. Maggie stood there patiently, her tail giving a slow, steady wag, as if to say, 'Thank you, my dear friend.'

I thought about all the deadly chemicals coursing through my body, the endless parade of tests, needles and prodding that had become my new routine. It felt cruel, relentless—like a battle fought on a field I hadn't chosen. Yet here was Maggie, her own body quietly under siege, enduring the same silent enemy with a grace I couldn't fathom. She didn't need a cocktail of therapies or a team of white coats; her contentment rested entirely in Tucker's gentle care. The attentive licks, the watchful eyes, the unspoken bond—they were her medicine. And somehow, they seemed more powerful than anything a pharmacy could ever produce.

In that moment, I couldn't decide if I was awed or devastated. Maybe both. Tucker's spa therapy was uncomplicated, pure and unburdened by the knowledge of what was coming. He didn't calculate prognosis or weigh outcomes. He just loved her, fully and without condition.

My silent, teary reflection was abruptly broken by the sound of Wes's voice, soft and steady, pulling me back to the room. 'Merry Christmas, Lovey,' he said, his words landing gently but with the force of a thunderclap.

Merry Christmas...

Two simple, beautiful words. Words that should evoke joy, tenderness and the warm embrace of a holiday wrapped in lights and love. Instead, they unraveled me. Like a dam bursting under the weight of too much water, emotion flooded forth—grief, loss, sorrow, a tidal wave of painful introspection. Expectation collided violently with reality, spinning me into an eddy from which I couldn't escape. Merry Christmas? How? Why? I had completely forgotten.

I was hollowed by the very sentiment that should have been a sweet balm. Instead of vitality and wonder, it felt like my soul had been eviscerated, leaving behind a raw, hopeless puddle of grief. I should feel happy, I thought. I should lean into the magic of the season, the sacredness of the day. But the gap between what I should feel and what I did feel was wide as a canyon, leaving me marooned in an emotional wasteland.

I should have known it was coming. The days leading to this moment were fraught with distress signals, little cracks in the armor of the season that hinted at the emotional landslide lurking, waiting to bury me. The loudest signal came from my daughter's Facebook post—a beautiful photograph of her boyfriend's family—everyone decked out in coordinating Buffalo Bill gear, glowing with happiness and warmth, the kind of photo that screams, 'This is what family should look like!'

They looked so... close. So intertwined. She had the prettiest smile, radiant and effortless. They all did, like a living Christmas—tinsel, bulbs, lights and all. It was crushing. The girl in that photo, my daughter, slips in and out of my life like a comet streaking through the night sky—rare, dazzling, and gone before I can even make a wish. Even now, with my sickness and an uncertain prognosis, I see shooting stars more often than I see her.

Then there's my middle son, just wrapping up his five-year tour in the Marines. He's moved hundred miles away, cementing a permanent distance between us. He's burned through months of vacation time, not once choosing to come home. My heart aches to see him, to wrap my arms around him, to anchor him here for even a moment. We talk often, and I know he loves me in his own way, but home seems to offer him... nothing.

And my oldest—my beautiful, complicated firstborn. Our relationship is a minefield, treacherous and unpredictable, scattered with the remnants of a war neither of us asked to fight. Years of mental illness, institutionalization and a broken behavioral health system have left scars on both of us. Guilt bombs, the weight of protection orders, the tangled mess of love and pain—it's all there, decorating our relationship with some twisted, nightmarish version of a holiday garland.

So there it is—my Merry Christmas portrait, in all its dysfunctional glory. This mess is the reality I live and the tangled masterpiece I carry with me.

My heart is heavy, my soul battered, but I'm standing. And maybe that's enough. Maybe that's what Christmas is about—embracing chaos, leaning into imperfections, and finding light in the places you least expect.

'Sometimes grief comes as the autumn leaf, unspoken, yet rain-washed, for the tears gather silently, not knowing how to speak.'

— Jayita Bhattacharjee

QUIET KIND OF BRAVE

I didn't slay a dragon.
I didn't even make the bed.
But I got up. I breathed.
I didn't cry when the junk drawer jammed.
And sometimes,
that's brave enough for now.

CHAPTER 20: WHEN LIFE GIVES YOU LEMONS... YOU CRY IN THE PRODUCE AISLE

When life gives you lemons, make lemonade—this maxim is a little too optimistic for my taste. Let's be honest, sometimes life hands you lemons the size of Volkswagens, and instead of thinking about sugar and water, you stand in the middle of the produce aisle, ugly-crying in front of a citrus pyramid.

My cancer diagnosis has me riding an emotional rollercoaster with no safety bar. One minute I'm affixing a 'You got this!' fake tattoo on my wrist (2:00 a.m. impulse buy), and the next, I'm Googling 'how to prepare for chemo' while eating unhealthy amounts of rice pudding straight from an industrial size container. My misery loves rice pudding.

The other day, I went to the grocery store to just get out of the house and clear my mind. Big mistake. I stared at a pile of lemons—bright, cheerful, gorgeous, mocking lemons—when it hit me like a sack of potatoes: I'm terrified. Afraid of chemo, the unknown toll, of

losing my long hair that I've loved for so many years (though it makes me look much older). And desperately afraid of leaving my family.

There I was, in the middle of this fluorescent-lit battlefield, whispering, 'Stupid lemons!' What else could I say? There's no Pinterest-worthy life hack for turning cancer into a sweet, sunshiny libation; I've googled it. Even my dear Amish friends told me about a lemon cure involving a daily glass of a whole pulverized lemon, a dash of honey and a permanent sourpuss. (Spoiler alert: it didn't work.)

A beautiful young woman glided past me with a cart full of kale and smiled like she had answers. I wanted to stop her and say, 'Excuse me, ma'am, but have you ever turned a lemon into a chemo survival plan? No? Didn't think so.' Instead, I smiled back, because I'm a polite train wreck.

The sad truth is, life's lemons don't come with instructions. There's no manual for navigating a cancer diagnosis or the angst that comes with it. So, what should I do with this Everest of life's lemons?

Well, for starters, I let myself cry in the produce aisle if I need to. I let myself feel scared, angry and overwhelmed, because denying it won't make it go away.

Then, once I've had my moment (or until I'm asked to leave the store), I grab those lemons, stick them in my cart, and figure out what the heck I'm going to do with so many stupid lemons. Maybe I'll make lemonade... Maybe I'll Martha-Stewart them into a lemon meringue pie. Or maybe I'll chuck them into the trash and order a pizza.

I guess I'm learning to drink it all in, one lemon at a time. Some days that means crying, other days laughing at the absurdity. And on the best days, believing something sweet might still come from the sour.

So, here's to lemons, tears and a little harmo-lemony. If you see me crying in the produce aisle, grab a cart and join me. Life's better with company and some tang.

'How beautiful is the rain! After the dust and heat, in the broad and fiery street, in the narrow lane, how beautiful is the rain!'

— Henry Wadsworth Longfellow

THE STORM TEACHES

The rain taught me to soften.
To stop cursing the clouds
and start planting in mud.
To bloom in strange places.
To let the flood
carry off
what I was never meant to hold.

CHAPTER 21: LIGHTS IN THE SKY AND HOLDING BACK PAIN

I hate loud sounds. Always have. A sudden boom flips a switch in my brain and sends me into full-blown irrational panic—not the 'I missed an episode of *The Bear*' kind, but the 'grab a life vest, we're going down' kind.

So no surprise, fireworks have never been my thing. They're loud, chaotic and rarely worth the hassle of parking, crowds and cold December nights in small-town Pennsylvania.

I live in farm country, where downtown is a church, a firehall and a community clinic. That's it. No stoplight—just a two-way stop sign and a handful of hitching posts for the Amish horses. Yes, you read that right. Hitching posts.

Welcome to beautiful, rural Pennsylvania, where the charm is winsome and the Wi-Fi is feckless.

Now, while I was recovering from chemo one quiet night, I had no clue the town was hosting its grand 'Community Christmas Walk'—which, to clarify, is a three-building loop across the street. And apparently, this included fireworks.

I was lying motionless in my dark quiet room when the first boom hit. The dogs flew across the floor, my bucket went airborne and I shot upright like a startled squirrel. I was fully awake, trying to process the information; adrenaline coursing through my veins as though a bear was chasing me for its dinner. I looked into the dark night at the grand pyrotechnic display spreading out in front of me. The sky outside my window exploded with color. Reds, blues, golds lit up the night as if the display had been planned just for me. My heart was racing, my mind spinning, but then suddenly something shifted.

My breath slowed. The panic softened. And for the first time in a long time, I wasn't afraid of the noise. I watched the sky light up and felt something else. Awe. Wonder. A flicker of peace inside the chaos.

Turns out, beauty doesn't always whisper. Sometimes it arrives loud, blazing and impossible to ignore.

Recently, a dear friend said to me, 'So many of us have silent pain that doesn't show up in holiday posts and pictures.' That single sentence stopped me cold.

Because she was right. We scroll through the glossy holiday photos—the glowing trees, the matching pajamas, the smiling faces—but we rarely see what's just outside the frame. The arguments. The empty chairs. The weight of unspoken grief. The spaces left by those who are no longer with us. That kind of ache doesn't pose well for pictures, but it's there. Oh, it's there. And sometimes, just knowing we aren't alone in it... matters more than anything.

After writing the earlier chapter A Merry and Messy Christmas, I cried for twenty-four hours straight. I mean ugly-cried—the kind of sobbing I reserve for the most catastrophic events, like John Denver dying, when my son left for the Marines, or when my first alpaca crossed the rainbow bridge (rest in peace, you magnificent fleece monster).

The thing is, I've built an impressive emotional dam over the years. I'm practically the Army Corps of Engineers when it comes to not crying. Need someone to mop the deck of a crab boat mid-storm to avoid feelings? I'm your girl. But this time, my dam broke.

And maybe that's okay. Maybe someone else needs to hear this as well.

There's something profoundly powerful in realizing your messiness mirrors someone else's. That in sharing the tangled threads of your story, you help others find the courage to untangle theirs.

Big emotion is hard. It's messy. It's unwelcome at dinner parties. But I'm learning. Slowly, awkwardly, that when we let the waters rise, they sometimes carve out space for something new to grow.

So, if you're holding pain that hasn't made it into the photo albums, know this: you're not alone. And you're deeply, fiercely, beautifully seen.

PART

FOUR:

ABSURDITY

IS A

SURVIVAL

SKILL

It started with a laugh I didn't mean to let out.

One of those surprised, snorty ones that slips past your defenses and escapes into the room like it owns the place. I don't even remember what triggered it—some absurd moment in the middle of an otherwise serious day. But I remember how it felt. Like oxygen. Like someone cracked open a window in a too-tight room.

That laugh didn't solve anything. It didn't change the diagnosis or reverse time or fix whatever had gone sideways that week. But it just diffused the tension for a moment and gave me space to breathe. And a brief respite is all that we need sometimes.

From there on, the world seemed to lean a little more off-kilter. Or maybe I just started noticing how funny it's always been. The universe has a wicked sense of humor, after all. The timing. The irony. The conversations you overhear in hospital waiting rooms. The way chaos arrives, looking like a flamingo in a tuxedo, expecting you to keep a straight face.

These pages are what followed. A collection of the offbeat, the sideways, the completely bonkers moments that somehow made everything feel more survivable. These aren't just stories—they're buoyant little life rafts. Strange, awkward, occasionally inappropriate and kind of miraculous in their own way.

If you find yourself laughing in the middle of something that isn't funny, welcome. You're doing it right.

THE SKY
HAS OPINIONS

The sky threw shade in drizzle form,
A moody sigh, both wet and warm.
I took it as a compliment,
Because I'm delusional and slightly bent.

CHAPTER 22: THE SOUND OF STILLNESS (LESSONS FROM AN AMISH PORCH)

My Amish friend Emma is the kind of person who can speak volumes without uttering a word. She doesn't rush to fill silences or compete for airspace. She makes space to listen; the kind of listening that makes you feel like your words matter. It's not performance. It's presence.

We didn't plan to have a deep conversation that night. We were just sitting, watching the rhythm of her world unfold: a grandson chasing chickens, a buggy creaking its way down the lane, the soft clatter of dishes being dried in the kitchen. But somewhere between a shared smile and the last sliver of sunset, I realized something: I was being heard.

Not analyzed. Not pitied. Not fixed. Just... heard.

That porch, with its uneven floorboards and well-worn cushions, became a retreat. And Emma, without saying much at all, became my guide.

In a world that rewards noise, she offered quiet. In a culture that

'The rain began again. It fell heavily, easily, with no meaning or intention but the fulfillment of its own nature, which was to fall and fall.'

— Helen Garner

insists on response, she offered understanding . And in doing so, she reminded me of something we all crave—someone to just sit beside us, in silence or story, without trying to rearrange the pieces.

In a world filled with noise, constant social media, endless notifications and relentless chatter, it seems like we've forgotten the simple, powerful art of listening. Truly listening. The kind where you aren't just preparing your feedback but instead are absorbing another person's words, thoughts and feelings.

Emma embodies this rare skill better than anyone I've ever met. She doesn't Google. She doesn't half-listen while scrolling through a phone. She asks questions—thoughtful, purposeful and resourceful. And when you answer, she gives you her full attention, as though your words are the only thing that matter in that moment.

'May I ask you a question?' is her signature opening line, delivered with such politeness and sincerity that it's impossible not to respond. Once, in a hospital waiting area, I watched Emma turn a roomful of weary strangers into a chorus of storytellers, all eager to share their experiences. It wasn't a performance or a tactic to pass the time. It was Emma being Emma—curious, engaged and fully present.

Her approach is deceptively simple but profoundly rare: ask, then listen.

A visit to Emma's home feels like stepping back in time to a world where the rush of modern life simply doesn't exist. Her back porch, a haven of simplicity, overlooks a stretch of peaceful woods that seem to exhale calm. Birdhouses hang in clusters, offering tiny homes to fluttering visitors, while her beloved squirrel feeders invite nature's busiest creatures. The smoke from the outdoor wood stove curls upward, carrying the scent of warmth and home. The walls are lined with vintage cookware, their polished surfaces catching the light, whispering stories of meals shared and memories made. Coffee cups line every available surface, a testament to the endless stream of visitors who find themselves here. Handcrafted rockers invite you to sit, to listen, to just be.

To visit Emma is to sit and talk. Not the hurried, distracted exchanges we've grown used to, but deep, meaningful conversation. The kind where you truly see the other person, hear them and respond in kind. It's simple, quiet, unassuming. Just pure connection in the woods.

Her questions are thoughtful and intentional. She asks not out of politeness but out of genuine curiosity and care. And when she listens, you feel it. You feel seen, valued and understood. When I'm on that porch, time slows, and the outside world fades away.

Emma's ways are different. Slower, quieter and infinitely more meaningful. She listens with her whole self, eyes focused, body leaning in, as though your words are carefully collected treasures. She doesn't jot things down or file them away on a device. Instead, she stores them in her vast memory bank, a repository of names, stories and details she'll recall with startling clarity years later. The connections Emma builds linger long after the conversation ends. You leave her home not just feeling heard, but feeling whole, as though the simple act of talking with her has restored a piece of yourself you didn't realize was missing.

I've started to realize how much we've lost by forgetting this art. We live in a world that amplifies the loudest voices, where being heard often feels more important than hearing. We multitask through conversations, formulating our responses before the other person has even finished speaking. We skim, scroll and react without really processing what's being said.

So, here's what Emma has taught me and what I'm still learning: Listening isn't passive. It's not just what you do while waiting for your turn to talk. It's a choice. A discipline. An act of love and respect.

So the next time someone speaks to you, try it. Put the phone down. Let the silence breathe. Ask a genuine question, then really hear the answer.

Because in a world that's shouting over itself, the art of listening might be the most valuable gift we can offer each other.

THE RAIN REMEMBERS

Rain doesn't fix what's broken.
It just reminds you
you're not the only one
falling apart
and learning how to live.

E mma doesn't just walk into a room—she enters it like a friendly detective on a mission from God. And if you're lucky enough to be in her line of sight, chances are you're about to receive a very polite but utterly disarming, 'May I ask you a question?'

What follows could be a query about your life, your health, the price of carrots, or how your people go about curing warts. And no matter your answer, she'll soak it in like it is the one missing page in The Manual of Life that she's writing.

Emma seems like she's from another century—but not in a dusty, distant way. She's fully alive, fully present and curious to the marrow. She runs a household, teaches children, administers healing salves, raises chickens, organizes weddings, and somewhere in between, she finds time to ask perfect strangers things most of us would never dare say out loud.

Her curiosity isn't nosy—it's holy. It's the kind that builds bridges, that dignifies the details of someone else's story, that turns a hospital waiting room into a gathering space of unfiltered humanity. To her, a stranger isn't a threat or an inconvenience—it's a mystery waiting to be gently and respectfully unraveled.

So, when one of our Amish friends (you guessed it—Emma) found herself in need of a hospital visit, Wes and I put on our chauffeur hats and loaded up the car. We were expecting a long night. What we got instead was a front-row seat to an unexpected masterclass in human connection... starring one very curious, very kind and endlessly surprising woman who decided the ER was as good a place as any to hold informal interviews with the sick and weary.

What happened next was well, absurd. And kind of beautiful.

CHAPTER 23: AN AMISH EMERGENCY (HAPPY HOUR AT THE ER)

When you live in rural Northwestern Pennsylvania, a trip to the ER is rarely an ordinary affair. Add an Amish friend to the mix, and it transforms into something straight out of a small-town sitcom, complete with cultural collisions, quiet resilience and more than a few moments of unexpected humor.

The Amish typically don't rush to hospitals. They tend to rely on home remedies, prayer and an impressive tolerance for pain. But once, Emma was experiencing pain beyond the reach of Epsom salts and a dandelion tincture. Wes and I are fluent in the art of Amish chauffeur duty, emergencies included.

At the hospital, the cultural contrasts became glaringly apparent. The waiting room was crowded like a bus station on the eve of a long weekend, teeming with unhappy patients, ill-behaved children running amok, and assorted family dramas unfolding by the minute. Yet for some reason, the initial sight of Amish people quiets a room. People stop what they're doing and stare inquisitively at the plain-clothed time-travelers, straight out of an old Western movie.

154

Emma is the kind of person who makes you feel like you've stepped into a simpler, more grounded world the moment you meet her. She's a walking encyclopedia of homeopathic healing, a local expert in burn treatments and remedies, and a teacher by day who somehow finds time to be a high-achieving homemaker around the clock. Her matriarchal role is deeply respected and together with her husband, they stand as pillars of their family and extended Amish community.

What sets her apart, even more than her vast knowledge, is her inquisitive nature. While we 'English' might rely on AI to answer life's questions, my friend asks, processes, learns and stores information in her *mind*—imagine that! She thrives on understanding people, places and ideas, often walking right up to a stranger and starting a conversation with her signature, 'May I ask you a question?'

Her warmth and confidence shine through in every interaction. Whether she's sharing a remedy for a stubborn burn or asking a shopkeeper about a peculiar item on their shelf, her presence is magnetic. She represents the essence of her community: resourceful, kind and deeply connected to the world around her.

This trip to the ER would soon prove to be a unique one. After we settled in for what promised to be a long wait, Emma's eyes began scanning the room, her curiosity bubbling to the surface. I could almost see the questions piling up in her mind like raindrops on a windowpane. There was so much to observe, so much to learn in this room filled with strangers—and so much time to do it.

She began with the person sitting beside her, leaning in kindly. 'May I ask, what brings you here?' she inquired , her voice warm and genuine. The lady answered, offering a polite but brief explanation, and before I knew it, they were deep in conversation. My friend's sincere interest turned that sterile waiting room into a space of connection.

She was just getting started. Soon, her attention shifted to the family sitting across from us, their wide-eyed child staring intently with a mixture of fascination and hesitation. I could almost hear the child's inner monologue: *Should I or should I not be talking to this stranger?*

Emma had no such reservations. She offered the child a kind smile, and in no time, her delightful personality broke through their defenses. The little one, now completely enchanted, leaned forward to answer questions and even asked a few of her own. Watching the exchange was like witnessing magic—Emma's ability to connect with people of all ages, in any setting, was nothing short of extraordinary.

By this time, curious onlookers began to take notice. The waiting room had transformed into a stage, with various conversations as the main performance. The actors were completely unaware of their growing audience. But the fascination was palpable. Surely, others harbored their own curiosities and silent inquiries. Don't we all? Yet, how many of us would have the confidence to ask a complete stranger, *'What brings you to the ER?'* Certainly not I.

But my friend wasn't just curious—she was genuinely concerned for each one of her new acquaintances.

Soon, the unspoken tension of the room gave way to intrigue. Rising from her seat with the poise of someone hosting a community meeting, she began moving from chair to chair, family to family, each encounter initiated with her trademark: 'May I ask you why you're here?'

One by one, stories emerged—some brief, others detailed. A young man nursing a swollen hand from a stubborn fight with a tool, an elderly couple quietly awaiting news from the back, a worried mother with a feverish toddler on her lap. Emma listened intently to every word, her questions precise yet compassionate, her interest authentic and caring.

It was extraordinary—a turn of events no one in that waiting room could have predicted. People seemed almost relieved and eager to share their stories, perhaps feeling a little less invisible in the sterile space where time always drags. Emma turned an ordinary, uncomfortable experience into a tapestry of human connection drawn in by the courage and warmth of someone who dared to do what most of us wouldn't.

It was, in every sense of the word, unforgettable.

CHAPTER 24: LOST IN TRANSLATION (ONE FRONT DOOR)

In rural life, there are spoken contracts, and then there are the unspoken ones—the kind sealed with a nod, a calloused handshake, and a mutual understanding that things will 'just work out.' Until they don't.

Years ago, Wes and I embarked on what we thought was a simple home improvement project. We hired an Amish man—known more for his silence than his blueprints—to build a breezeway connecting our house to the garage. There were no drawings. No contracts. Just a vague description, a mutual squint toward the future, and what we now recognize as a wildly optimistic verbal agreement.

The trouble began immediately. Something about the roof pitch, or the frame, or maybe the foundation. Honestly, I stopped listening after Wes started explaining things in that low drone that sounds suspiciously like the teacher from the Peanuts cartoons: 'Waaa waaa wall joist waaa slope angle waaa...' And yet, somehow, Wes, the Amish builder, and his horse all nodded in solemn agreement, as if a blueprint had been silently transmitted through barn telepathy.

The next day, Wes returned home to find windows installed at a height that could only be appreciated by giraffes or very determined squirrels. Once again, man and builder stood eye to eye (give or take a beard), trying to negotiate their way back to architectural sanity.

Eventually, after several more rounds of invisible contracts and unintelligible standoffs, Wes hit his limit. He declared the gentleman's agreement officially null and void and announced he'd finish the job himself.

That evening, we went out for dinner, hoping to shake off the stress of the doomed breezeway. But when we returned, we noticed something strange. The front of the house looked... off.

'Did we leave the door open?' I asked.

Wes squinted. 'No. We... we left the door.'

Indeed, our front door was gone. Vanished. No signs of forced entry—just a neatly placed pile of hardware on the floor, like an exhibit in a very quiet, very passive-aggressive art installation. The Amish builder, it turns out, had returned while we were out and reclaimed what he felt was still owed: one standard entry door, minus hinges and knob.

Wes drove straight to his house, doorless but determined. What happened during that final exchange remains a mystery, but somehow, they reached a peace agreement. The door returned, the breezeway remained half-finished, and a lesson was learned: in rural Pennsylvania, payment plans may be measured in pine and paneling.

Years later, the story took one final twist. Wes discovered that the friend who had driven the Amish man to repossess our door was, in fact, someone we knew.

'You drove him where?' Wes asked, incredulous. 'And you didn't stop him?'

The friend simply shrugged. 'I figured he had his reasons.'

And maybe he did. Maybe everyone did.

Looking back, it's these strange, almost folkloric episodes that reveal the true quirks of small-town life. Where misunderstandings don't come from malice but from mismatched assumptions. Where translation can be lost not just in language, but in tone, timing, and the cost of one missing front door.

But somehow, amid the confusion, a few laughs, and some slightly bruised pride, friendships endured. And if that's not worth a door, I don't know what is.

RAIN HAIR, DON'T CARE

My hair in rain becomes a crown,
Of chaos draped in wilted brown.
But thunder doesn't seem to mind—
It claps for me, so I feel fine.

CHAPTER 25: MY DREAMS DESERVE AN OSCAR

One day, my Amish friend casually mentioned, 'I had a dream I rode a horse.'

'Oh, that's so nice!' I replied. 'I dreamt I was an international Chinese spy working to dismantle a top-secret underground organization bent on world domination.'

She blinked at me, expressionless, the way Amish people do when they are trying to decide if I need prayer or an exorcism. And in that quiet pause, I had a moment of self-reflection: why are my dreams so... extra?

I've always loved dreaming. My dreams aren't just random nonsense but full-blown, Hollywood-level productions. I dream in color, with dialogue, original soundtracks, and plotlines that resolve like someone in my brain actually cares about structure. My subconscious, apparently, is a screenwriter with a union job and excellent benefits.

And they're funny. Way funnier than anything I say while awake. I wake up thinking, *how am I this clever in my sleep, yet fully conscious, I sometimes forget how to spell February?*

A recurring favorite: I am an international spy fluent in Mandarin.

I know this because I understand everything and everyone seems very impressed. I am always dressed impeccably—silk robes for secret rooftop meetings, sleek suits for airport scenes. The spy wardrobe alone deserves an award.

My dreams also involve me smuggling mysterious, high-tech gadgets past airport security. What do the gadgets do? No idea. But I know the fate of the free world depends on getting them past TSA inside a ramen noodle pack or disguised as a travel pillow.

But it's not all espionage and glory. There are plenty of dreams where I am just deeply, profoundly humiliated.

Like the one where I'm leading a boardroom meeting in a lovely green blouse and suddenly, my Spanx explodes. Not tear. Not roll. Explode. One second I'm speaking confidently, and the next, I'm flailing like a trapped sea creature while a coworker calmly observes, 'Wow, those things really work.'

Then there was the dream where I met God.

We were standing under a massive marble rotunda, surrounded by galaxies and angels swirling in perfect harmony. The floor shimmered like a living map of the universe. I asked, 'What is this?'

God said, 'It's a map of Heaven.'

And of course, the first thing out of my mouth was, 'Where does John Denver live?'

God smiled. 'Oh, almost heaven. He's on the country roads.'

Was it literal? Poetic? Did John Denver have a heavenly cabin with a banjo on his lap? God didn't say. He just gave me that all-knowing look, and I decided to let it go.

WHY IS DREAM ME SO BRILLIANT?

This is what gets me. Dream Me is multilingual, stylish, fearless. Awake Me knocks over my coffee and forgets what I walked into the room for.

Shouldn't some of that brilliance leak into my daytime brain? But no. Instead, I stumble through my to-do list waiting to return to the place where I'm secretly running covert operations in a silk kimono.

MY DREAMS DESERVE AN OSCAR

I've made peace with it. My dreams are more compelling than my real life. And maybe that's not sad—it's sacred. It's my imagination stretching its wings in the only place where it doesn't feel self-conscious.

I keep a notebook on my nightstand. Not just to mine ideas for stories, but because I believe my dreams are trying to tell me something about who I'm becoming.

So if you dream about a horse, I'll cheer for you. I'll be over here evading enemy agents in Shanghai, slipping laser devices past TSA, and doing it all in heels. Not because I'm chasing some fantasy version of myself—but because deep down, I think my subconscious already knows who I am becoming.

And honestly? She's kind of a badass.

PART FIVE: PUDDLES, OAKS AND WHAT REMAINS

I am a pluviophile, a lover of rain. There is something about it that soothes the soul and stirs the imagination all at once. Rain slows the world down just enough for us to notice it again—the scent of wet pavement, the hush of a cloudy sky, the way time lingers a little longer between drops. I have cried in the rain, laughed under it and sat quietly while it said the things I could not. To me, rain has never just been weather. It has been company.

Rain is where memories return and creativity wakes up. It is the perfect backdrop for writing, painting or just sitting still. Even puddles feel poetic—once avoided, now joyfully jumped into. Somewhere between the gray skies and the glisten on the sidewalk, rain reveals what we usually rush past: the shimmer in the mundane, the ache we have been carrying, the beauty in not having everything figured out.

Most people chase the sun. I have learned to welcome the rain. It softens the noise, resets the mood and reminds me that growth happens in the storm, not just in the spotlight. Rain does not ask us to be strong. It just asks us to keep breathing. And some days, that is more than enough.

CHAPTER 26: FORECAST: CLOUDY WITH A CHANCE OF FOLKLORE

There's a particular kind of silence just before the rain arrives in a small town. It's not the heavy expectant hush of a coastal storm or the eerie stillness of an incoming thunderclap. No, this silence is gentler—like a town pausing mid-sentence to take a deep breath.

You can feel it in the way the leaves tremble. In the scent of damp earth rising before the first drop even lands. The air thickens—not unpleasantly but with a quiet weight that says something familiar is on its way. Not just rain but rhythm. Life slowing down. Settling in.

That's the beauty of small-town living. It moves at its own tempo. Some might call it slow or predictable but I've come to love the poetry of it—the way tractors rumble through town, steady and sure. The way Amish buggies clip-clop along the shoulders, their drivers nodding to the cars behind them. The way porches turn into theaters for the daily parade—rocking chairs creaking, dogs barking, kids dashing barefoot across yards. Even the ducks do laps around the neighborhood like they're on patrol.

Here, news travels faster than UPS. A fresh coat of paint on a front door sparks three serious conversations and half a dozen theories before sundown.

And rain? Rain isn't an inconvenience here. It's an occasion. The scent alone sends people into motion. Farmers check their fields. Shopkeepers pull in signs. Laundry disappears off lines in one practiced swoop. It's not a question of if it will rain but when, how long and whether the dirt roads will hold or turn to chocolate pudding.

But more than that, rain invites stillness. People pause. They lean back, slow down, make space. Because maybe there's nowhere urgent to be. Or maybe folks around here just know—rain has its own stories to tell.

Stories of childhood afternoons chasing puddles. First kisses stolen under eaves. Whispered confessions beneath tin roofs while the water drums above.

That's what I love most about this place—how even the simplest moments feel like they hold a whole life inside them. The rain falls on streets it's known for generations, carrying laughter, loss and the quiet enduring beauty of everyday lives.

So when the first drops hit the sidewalk, I lean back, coffee in hand and listen. Because here, even the rain has something to say.

And then just when you think you've settled into the quiet, life reminds you it has a sense of humor. If life had a soundtrack, it wouldn't be a perfect symphony. It would be a mash-up of drum solos, cowbells and an unexpected kazoo solo no one agreed on. Just when you think you've got the beat—boom, the tempo changes and you're flailing like a cat in a bathtub.

And yet somehow, we dance.

Not always well. Some days it's a graceful waltz. Other days, its interpretive chaos fueled by caffeine and stubborn hope. But the music plays and the only real mistake is standing still.

I used to think resilience meant standing tall, bracing for storms, refusing to budge. But I've come to believe that real resilience is learning to laugh in the rain. To find humor in the mess. To stop trying to dodge every raindrop and start splashing like a kid who forgot to care what people think.

Some of the best things in life happen when everything goes sideways. A detour that leads to something beautiful. A conversation that turns hilarious without warning. A plan that falls apart and leaves room for joy you didn't see coming.

Yes, life is messy. It rains when we want sun. We step in puddles. We lose umbrellas. But maybe the goal isn't control. Maybe it's wonder.

Because the rain will fall. That part's not optional. What we do with it—that's the story.

So, when the next storm comes, I hope I remember to step out into it. To feel it. To let it wash something clean. And if I end up soaked—well, at least I'll have a great story to tell.

'*How beautiful it is outside when everything is wet from the rain— before, in, and after the rain. I oughtn't to let a single shower pass.*'

— Vincent van Gogh

CHAPTER 27: FROM ROOTS TO RIPPLES (THE GRACE OF OAKS AND PUDDLES)

The other day, a friend and I were talking about reincarnation. You know, the classic 'What would you come back as if you could choose anything?' question. She didn't hesitate for a second: 'The Angel Oak,' she said confidently, referring to the majestic tree in Charleston with its centuries of wisdom and sprawling branches.

It was a solid choice. Noble, timeless, grand.

My answer was a little... different.

'I'd come back as a puddle,' I said.

She blinked at me, completely baffled. 'A puddle? Why on earth would you want to be a puddle?

'And that's where this story begins...

In Charleston, South Carolina, there's a tree unlike any other. The Angel Oak, a sprawling live oak with twisting limbs and roots that seem to stretch forever, has stood for over 500 years. Imagine that—five centuries of life, quietly observing the changing world.

This tree has witnessed everything from settlers arriving in wagons creaking under the weight of hopes and dreams to raging wars that plowed the land before fading quietly into history. The tree has shaded picnickers beneath its sprawling canopy, absorbing laughter blended with the rustling leaves and stood solemn as lovers etched their initials into its bark, their whispered promises tucked safely into its bark. Countless storms have drenched its roots, lightning splitting the sky above, its branches swaying and groaning, yet it stands like an ancient sentinel.

If the Angel Oak could speak, I imagine it would talk most fondly about the simple, fleeting moments—children laughing as they climb its limbs, the tickling feathers of birds nesting in its branches or the way the sunlight filters through its leaves after a rainstorm. The Angel Oak, with its vast canopy and centuries of life, has seen it all. It is a testament to resilience, strength and the quiet grace of simply existing through time's endless march. It doesn't strive or demand recognition. It just is, rooted in purpose: offering shade, beauty and history to anyone who stops to notice.

You'd think, given the magnificence of this tree, that if I were to be reincarnated, I'd aspire to come back as something equally grand—an enduring oak, a towering redwood or something else with a deep, meaningful story to tell. But oddly enough, my aspirations are far simpler.

In my next life, I'd like to come back as a puddle.

Because, in a way, a puddle shares a similar purpose. Like the Angel Oak, it exists without pretense, offering its own small contribution to the world. It reflects, it nurtures and it invites others to pause and appreciate beauty in its fleeting existence.

Much like the Angel Oak, a humble puddle has its own unique perspective on the world, observing life from its lowly yet remarkable vantage point and reflecting boundless joy and untethered beauty.

On the surface, being a puddle sounds like the least glamorous gig in the reawakening line-up. You're basically a blob of water, stuck in a low spot, at the mercy of the elements and passersby. But think about it: a puddle gets to hold the sky in its surface, offering a glimpse of the heavens in a way that makes people stop and look twice. Puddles are unassuming yet endlessly useful, overlooked yet profoundly magnificent.

Imagine this: you're formed in the aftermath of a violent rainstorm, your edges shimmer as the clouds part, reflecting the fresh light of a newly washed world. You don't have to strive or hustle. Your purpose is simply... to be. Kids spot you, and their faces light up with glee. They jump, they splash and for a fleeting moment, you become the epicenter of pure enlightenment and joy.

Dogs come trotting by, pausing to sniff and cock their heads, momentarily puzzled by their own reflection rippling in your surface. They bark, leap and paw at the mysterious 'other dog,' adding their own chaos to your calm. And then there are the humans who tread a little too close, muddying the water and creating charming, swirling eddies.

Even oil spots, often seen as blemishes, gift you with their own kind of beauty—a kaleidoscope of mesmerizing peacock colors. You, a humble puddle, transform an ordinary sidewalk into an artist's canvas, a moment of unexpected wonder for those who seek.

Maybe life as a puddle isn't such a bad deal. You get to be playful, reflective and unapologetically yourself. You're not being a river or a lake. You're just a puddle, here for a good time, not a long time. Look at it from that perspective and you could learn a thing or two.

So, while many millions have gone before me toasting the great Angel Oak, I raise my glass to the magic of puddles; reminders to embrace the beauty of being right where we are, even if it gets a bit muddy. You don't need to control or resist. You simply exist, embracing the mess, the beauty and the joy of being perfectly imperfect.

The Angel Oak may stand tall, a testament to strength and longevity. But puddles are here to remind us that life isn't just about how long you last. It's about the moments you create while you're here. They may not endure for centuries, but their impact is immediate and undeniable—a reflection of the sky, a burst of laughter or even a muddy shoe that tells a story.

So here's to puddles, to fleeting beauty and to the messy, marvelous moments that make life worth living. In a world that so often demands greatness, sometimes it's enough to simply be.

'There are some things you learn best in calm, and some in storm.'

— Willa Cather, *The Song of the Lark*

CHAPTER 28: REDRAWING THE MAP OF ME

I don't think I've ever said it out loud before.

I have ALK-positive non-small cell lung cancer.

I am 56 years old.

And I have about a 32 percent chance of surviving the next five years.

There it is. Words that wound even as they escape my lips, slicing clean through the fabric of everything I thought I knew about my life. It feels as if someone stabbed me with a proverbial knife and left it there, not a quick cut, not a mercy blow, but a slow, agonizing hemorrhaging. A wound that I am somehow expected to dress and bandage while pretending I'm still whole.

If there were a scale for measuring the luck of cancer patients—a twisted, demented carnival game where even the winners lose—you can say I'm one of the 'lucky' ones.

Cleveland Clinic's finest caught it just in time, if there is such a thing. A third of my lung was cut away with precision, a handful of lymph nodes evicted, though not before they wreaked their quiet devastation inside me, whispering of their plans to spread.

I survived the first act.

Now I live in the second.

I am held upright by a medical breakthrough—a daily, toxic lifeline designed to keep the cancerous cells from regrouping and launching a second war against my body. A 70-something percent chance it will work. A 100 percent chance that, while it fights, it will also slowly poison my liver and kidneys.

It is a delicate, wretched dance.

A tango between hope and destruction, choreographed by necessity, performed without applause.

There is a grief that comes long before the end.

It's the mourning of an imagined life—the one I thought I was living toward without even realizing it. The gentle, almost thoughtless way I counted on time to unfold. The quiet confidence that there would always be more years, more birthdays, more sunsets, more arguments, more reconciliations, more late-night laughs over nothing at all.

I grieve the woman I thought I'd get to become.

I grieve the slow, soft aging that I used to fear but had finally, almost, begun to look forward to—the kind where your skin tells a map of your joys and your eyes hold a lifetime of stories.

I grieve retirement plans we hadn't even fully made yet, beach trips we hadn't yet booked, holidays I just assumed would come like clockwork, year after year, tucked safely inside a life that felt ordinary, and therefore eternal.

I even grieve the arguments we never got around to having—the ridiculous ones about thermostat settings and whose turn it was to take out the trash—because only people who expect a lifetime together bother to debate such things.

And I grieve for the people who love me.

Because I know, with a bone-deep certainty, that one day they will carry a sorrow with my name on it.

And that thought is somehow worse than carrying my own.

There is a death before the death—the death of the future.

And learning to live inside that hollowed-out space is at times, unbearable.

And so, I live.

Not in the way I used to, though.

Not fully.

Maybe about 32 percent of me is still the woman I once was— the one who made plans without a second thought, who trusted her own body without reading it for signs of betrayal. That part still shines, sometimes. A stubborn flicker of the old light.

The rest of me feels like scattered remains—a fragile museum of what was and what isn't anymore. Some pieces are still bright, catching the light just so on a good day. A laugh that escapes without warning. A conversation that feels almost normal. A fleeting sense of being here that, for a moment, I forget.

But most of the pieces are darker now. Heavier.

I move through the world differently, carrying the weight of fear, uncertainty and the crushing knowledge that every 'next time' might have an expiration date stamped somewhere I can't see.

Each piece breathes in its own time.

Some days, it feels like a puzzle I am trying to assemble in the dark—hundreds of jagged emotional fragments, edges worn from handling, half-formed, never quite fitting the way they used to. I can piece some of those parts together. I can make out the vague shape of a life. But there are whole sections missing—spaces I can't seem to fill, no matter how hard I try.

Hope still exists here, but it's not the pure, polished kind.

It's cloudy. Murky.

A hand reaching up through water so dark you can't tell if it's waving or drowning.

I live inside that water now.

Treading, floating, sinking, surfacing... over and over again.

And somehow, even when it feels impossible, I keep breathing.

THE GRIEF TIDE

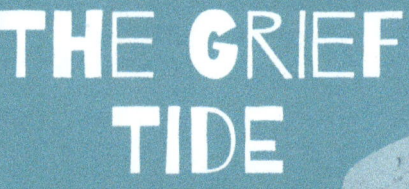

Grief doesn't knock.
It slips under the door.
It curls in your coffee,
Hides in the drawer.
But even waves that sting
Still smooth the shore,
And every tide that pulls
Will push once more.

'The rain continued.
It was a hard rain,
a perpetual rain, a
sweating and steaming
rain; it was a mizzle, a
downpour, a fountain,
a whipping at the eyes,
an undertow at the
ankles; it was a rain to
drown all rains and the
memory of rains.'

— Ray Bradbury, *The Long Rain*

Epilogue

As you reach the end of The Rain Whisperer, I hope you carry with you a spark of light from these pages—a reminder that even in the midst of life's fiercest storms, there is always room for laughter, reflection and hope.

This book was born from moments of vulnerability and unexpected humor, a testament to the resilience of the human spirit. Along our shared journey, we've discovered that every challenge, every downpour, and every twist of fate has the power to nurture growth and reveal hidden beauty. I've poured my heart into these essays, not to offer easy answers, but to celebrate the messy, unpredictable and ultimately enriching tapestry of life.

May you find solace in the gentle cadence of the rain, inspiration in the smallest droplets of joy and the courage to dance in your own storms. Remember, every ending is simply the start of a new chapter, and every storm gives way to clearer skies.

And as you step forward, I hope you embrace the beauty in life's simplest moments—the way rain softens the earth, the way laughter lightens the heaviest of days, the way love and friendship transform the most ordinary places into extraordinary ones. Because in the end, it's not just about surviving the storm; it's about finding the poetry within it.

Thank you for walking this path with me. May your days be filled with unexpected laughter, quiet wonder and the knowledge that even the darkest clouds can hold the promise of a brighter tomorrow.

'You can dance in the storm. Don't wait for the rain to be over before because it might take too long. You can do it now. Wherever you are, right now, you can start, right now; this very moment.'

— Israelmore Ayivor

About the Author

Christina Madonia-Knisley is a small-town satirist with a heart as big as her punchlines—one part Hallmark heroine, two parts Lucille Ball caught in a roundabout. From booping alpaca noses to blogging through cancer like its stand-up comedy, she turns life's messes into literary magic. She collects rainy days like others collect stamps, finds purpose in puddles, and writes like her keyboard is powered by espresso and emotional whiplash.

Her dogs are spoiled, her husband's a sitcom co-star and her greeting cards need therapy. Whether she's having deep chats with a velour-clad God, penning a love letter to her lungs (sarcastically), or launching a fake company just to make people laugh—she does it with grace, grit, and a grocery list of random hatreds (looking at you, sunshine and coffee creamer). Simply put: Christina is the kind of storyteller you'd want narrating your life... or at least roasting it with flair.

Acknowledgments

A very special thank you to my editor, Shradha Biyani, whose steady hand and sharp eye helped shape The Rain Whisperer. Shradha didn't just edit words—she listened between them. She gently guided the rhythm, preserved the heart, and polished the rough edges while honoring my voice every step of the way.

Her insight, patience, and care were instrumental in bringing these essays to life with clarity and grace. I am deeply grateful for her partnership, her professionalism, and her kindness throughout this entire journey.

About the Illustrator

Sasha Popova-Pluzhnyk is the extraordinary visual designer and illustrator who breathed artistic life into The Rain Whisperer. Born in Uzbekistan (her words: 'don't ask') in 1990, Sasha grew up as a tiny, sensitive girl in a 1990s post-Soviet Ukrainian industrial city—a place equal parts beautiful and criminal at the time, and somehow she still 'dances with the rain' amid the foreign invasion of her country. Somehow, all of those shades of absurdity equipped her perfectly to understand and illustrate my words with stunning depth and whimsy.

Armed with a degree in theory and history of arts, Sasha draws from a wide range of inspirations—from Ukrainian Suprematism and naive folk traditions to Matisse's papercutting—to create the perfect atmosphere for each project she touches. She is a dreamer. She is an essentialist. She is, quite simply, Sasha.

I am endlessly grateful for her vision, her talent, and for the magic she brought to this book.